# Divine Feminine Handbook

## Volume I

### Overcoming
### Self-Doubt

MARILYN PABON

**BALBOA.**PRESS

A DIVISION OF HAY HOUSE

Balboa Press books may be ordered through booksellers or by contacting:

Balboa Press
A Division of Hay House
1663 Liberty Drive
Bloomington, IN 47403
www.balboapress.com
844-682-1282

Print information available on the last page.

ISBN: 978-1-9822-6518-2 (sc)
ISBN: 978-1-9822-6519-9 (e)

Balboa Press rev. date:   03/26/2021

# INTRODUCTION

*"The privilege of a lifetime is to become
who you truly are." Carl Jung*

The world needs you to remember your Divinity. You are a special, wise soul who chose to come to earth at this time, bringing Divine Feminine wisdom with you, to help usher in a new world.

The Divine Feminine has a longing to be more, do more, find her purpose and how she can grow and contribute to the betterment of the world. The Divine Feminine is sacred and loving. There is no need to be afraid or put off when you hear reference to the Divine Feminine. This is not sorcery or an anti-male or an anti-God movement in any way. This is a loving, healing, compassionate, nurturing, intuitive, and creative force which exists within us all.

## Herstory (her-story)

Recent scientific investigations into prehistory suggest that there was a rich vein of feminine wisdom at the core of Western civilization. Due to technological advances in the fields of science and archaeology a wealth of new information about the past has come to light and is uncovering centuries of historical distortion to find original truth.

I believe that by knowing the ancient history of women you will better understand who you really are, where you come from and why you are here now. With this wisdom you will have a fierce awakening of your identity and divinity and never suffer from self-doubt again. Understanding our past helps us understand our present.

We are going to travel back to the beginning, beyond history to pre-history, and learn that women were originally seen as sacred and revered. We were the original leaders, healers and spiritual guides of the world.

We will travel through time and see how the masculine energy eventually overpowered the Divine Feminine and dominated her and Mother Earth for thousands of years, without any accountability. As a result, our future and the health of the planet hangs in the balance.

That brings us to our world today and our purpose for being on earth at this time. The Divine Feminine will bring ancient wisdom, corrective balance and compassion into the world for its healing.

## Ancient Wisdom

We live in a time with ancient wisdom at our fingertips and a multitude of ancient spiritual traditions from many cultures which are bursting forth in new forms for our Modern Age. We can bridge ancient beliefs and practices to match our modern sensibilities. I have included many of these ancient tools for you to use to further cultivate your intuitive Inner Goddess. It is time to bring ancient wisdom alive and heal ourselves and our world.

Our evolution is far from over. There is a new Divine Feminine energy flowing over the world, transforming us and showing us a new more inclusive, loving and creative direction. The world needs us to be soft as much as it needs us to be warriors.

Whether you are walking down the Goddess path for the first time, or you are already enjoying a sacred relationship with your Divine Feminine self, you will learn to eliminate self-doubt, find and fulfill your personal calling, and ultimately your inner happiness. We each have our own divine purpose and specialness which we need to find and contribute to the world, which will bring change in our own lives and the world around us.

- Have you lost faith in yourself to make good choices, like choosing the right guy or job or where to live?
- Do you doubt your gifts and talents are good enough to share or help others with?
- Is it hard for you to make decisions because you are afraid you will make the wrong one?
- Are you afraid to set boundaries because you fear losing love or friendships?
- Do you fear being disliked or having anyone mad at you?
- Do you avoid and dread confrontation for fear of losing the battle because you aren't able to defend or explain yourself as you would like to?
- Do you feel self-conscious about your looks, talents, education, etc?
- Do you doubt the belief system you grew up with or the path you are on?

If you identify with any of the above scenarios, that is all about to change after reading this book!

*"Divine Feminine Handbook"* is a four-book series:
*Volume I: Overcoming Self-Doubt*
*Volume II: Awakening Your Inner Goddess*
*Volume III: Divine Feminine Self-Care*
*Volume IV: Self Reliance in a Changing World*

# CONTENTS

# CHAPTER 1

## You are More Powerful Than You Have Ever Been Allowed to Believe

*"Never forget the power that flows in your veins.*
*Never forget you are medicine for the world."*

Like all habits, self-doubt can come from a wide variety of sources. And in fact, no two people's struggles with self-doubt are exactly the same. For example, for one person, self-doubt may have originated in childhood, perhaps as a result of the way they were raised. On the other hand, self-doubt can become an issue later in adulthood, in response to an unexpected crisis or stressor like divorce or job loss.

No one is immune to self-doubt and everyone has moments where they second-guess whether they have what it takes to overcome their challenges and achieve their ambitions. Yet as studies show, women tend to doubt themselves more and back themselves less than the men around them. Men are almost always more confident than women, even when the women are equally or more talented.

It begins early. By the age of 5, girls are less likely than boys to believe that they can be "really really smart." By middle school, girls have lower expectations for what they can achieve in their professional lives. And even women who are highly confident in their ability to rise to the same heights as their male peers experience a decline in confidence within a few years of entering the workforce.

## What are the up-sides of Self-Doubt?

For starters, self-doubt alerts you to the presence of fear. And of course, where there is fear there is also an opportunity for growth and development, which lies outside the confines of your comfort zone.

Secondly, self-doubt alerts you to the fact that you are lacking in something. For instance, you may lack resources, knowledge or experience to get a job done. As such, all you effectively need to do is identify what it is you are lacking, and then go out there and acquire those resources, knowledge, or get that experience or support required to subdue the self-doubt you are currently experiencing.

Thirdly, self-doubt essentially helps discourage complacency. Self-doubt makes us alert and aware of potential problems and pitfalls that may lie ahead. With this understanding in mind, we can make better decisions moving forward. Therefore, it's perfectly okay to doubt yourself when faced with uncertainty. It's not the doubt that will hinder you, but rather how you handle that self-doubt that makes all the difference in the end.

## Signs That You Struggle With Self-Doubt

What follows are some common signs or indicators that self-doubt is a problem in your life:

**Difficulty taking compliments.** If you consistently get anxious or ashamed whenever someone gives you a compliment, it could be a sign that you don't value yourself enough as a result of chronic self-doubt. Of course, compliments can sometimes be uncomfortable for anyone, but if you regularly struggle to take compliments and frequently avoid situations where you might be complimented, this could be a sign of a problem with self-doubt.

**Reassurance-seeking.** A habitual pattern of asking for reassurance when you're upset or having a hard time making decisions is frequently a sign of self-doubt issues. When you doubt your own abilities, it naturally produces anxiety. And the quickest way to alleviate anxiety is often to ask other people to make a decision or tell you things are okay. The problem is, this teaches your own mind that your judgment is not to be trusted, and in the long-run, this only intensifies your habit of self-doubt.

**Low self-esteem.** Many things can lead to low self-esteem, but by far one of the most common is self-doubt. When you regularly doubt and second-guess your own decisions and preferences, it's as if you had another person following you around all day telling you how dumb and untrustworthy you are. Even if you technically knew it wasn't true, the constant doubt and criticism would start to wear on you emotionally. And eventually, it would start to impact your entire identity and sense of self.

**Difficulty giving yourself credit.** Similar to having a hard time accepting compliments, if you regularly struggle to give yourself credit for a job well done or simply doing something nice, it could be a sign of self-doubt struggles. When the habit of self-doubt gets out of control, it tends to "squeeze out" any other responses and doubt simply becomes your default way of interpreting anything you do or achieve.

**Feeling like you're never good enough.** In some ways, this should be obvious, but if you consistently feel bad about yourself and consistently doubt your own abilities and achievements, maybe there's a correlation there. The trouble is, self-doubt, like many habits, can become so automatic and ingrained as to be almost invisible. But if doubting yourself becomes simply the water you swim in, it's hard to imagine how you could hope to feel good about yourself.

**Indecisiveness.** You consistently struggle to make even small decisions for fear of making the wrong decision and whatever consequences may result. Example: When you decide on a restaurant for dinner, then doubt the decision and worry about potential negative consequences, you produce a burst of anxiety. Then, in order to quickly alleviate that anxiety, you defer the decision to someone else which relieves you of the responsibility for the outcome and lessens your anxiety. Unfortunately, in the long-run, indecisiveness only erodes your self-esteem and confidence and makes your habit of self-doubt even stronger.

**You procrastinate.** Self-doubt is about letting inaction take over. When you are full of doubts, your willpower diminishes.

**You let over thinking silence the voice of your passion.** Stop allowing logic to drive your decisions. A life without uncertainty is not a life worth living. Those who are afraid of failing are afraid of living. Let your crazy-self be in the driver's seat from time to time.

**Fear.** We constantly hold ourselves back from doing the things we believe would bring true meaning and purpose into our lives because there's this constant fear that we're not good enough. Whether it's around our skills, abilities, personality, or the way we do things on a daily basis, self-doubt is always nagging us in the back of our minds.

Self-doubt shows up when we want to make a change in our lives. Maybe it's a better job, a different living situation, a healthier lifestyle, or a new relationship. There's always this feeling there must be more to life than how you're living right now. Yet you doubt you deserve to have the life you're dreaming of. You doubt you'll have the motivation, dedication, emotional stability, or perseverance to actually make it happen. You think of everything that could possibly go wrong instead of what could go right.

## Change Your Story

Everybody has a story. Your past has shaped you to be who you are today. But you also have stories that you make up in your mind. These stories come from things that have happened in the past. They come from things other people have criticized you for. They also come from assumptions about yourself and the future. You start to believe that these things are true no matter what. The thing is, you have the ability to rewrite your story. You get to decide who you want to be and what you do with your life.

## Ways to Overcome Self Doubt

**Change your environment:**
This means being more intentional about the people you spend time with, both at work and personally. That's repeatedly been shown to be a key to a longer life, too. You can make an argument that building the right community is crucial to everything: marketing, dealing with aging parents, divorce, and more.

**Stop caring about what other people think:**
Think about the 20-40-60 rule. Originally espoused by actress Shirley MacLaine and adhered to by Silicon Valley legend, entrepreneur and investor Heidi Roizen, the rule goes something like this:
"At 20, you are constantly worrying about what other people think of you. At 40 you wake up and say, 'I'm not going to give a damn what other people think anymore.' And at 60 you realize no one is thinking about you at all." The most important piece of

information there, Roizen says: "Nobody is thinking about you from the very beginning."

If people don't really care that much, then hyper-comparison can be reduced, and in turn so can self-doubt. Stop comparing yourself to others! You are enough. Allow yourself to be you.

**Research:**

Because self-doubt typically stems from a lack of understanding about your situation, sometimes all it takes is for you to do a little research to help you gain the certainty you need to take the next step along your journey.

**It is also helpful to share your doubts with others:**

When you share what you're uncertain about with other people, they will likely provide you with a fresh and unique perspective on the situation. As a result, you may begin to see the situation in a new and more positive light, which can help you make more optimal decisions moving forward.

In fact, certainty could just be a phone call away. Gain the support and guidance of the right person and they could very well help put this uncertain situation you are dealing with in its proper context.

**Remember your Divinity:**

More about that in the following chapters. The time has come for the Divine Feminine to rise up, help one another, stop competing and comparing, love each other and look out for each other. Changes will be made. Belief systems will evolve. Belief in yourself will return. Peace in your heart will return.

**Trusting yourself:**

You have to trust your intuition, your journey, your feelings, and the whole process that you're going through right now.

**Adjust our mind set:**

Once you realize that you have power within you, you can take responsibility for your life and your actions and do the scary things anyway. It all comes down to your mind set and whether you believe you are worthy of having the things in life that you want.

**Cultivate your sense of purpose.**

Having a well-cultivated set of values and strong sense of personal purpose is one of the best ways to free yourself from self-doubt. In fact, the very existence of chronic self-doubt may in fact be a symptom of a lack of strong purpose in your life. Often simply clarifying these values is enough to jumpstart a strong sense of purpose that will help pull you out of self-doubt and negative thinking. That is what this book is all about.

**Listen to your gut more often than not:**

Re-wild yourself. Relearn to trust your instinct and your passion. That doesn't mean to stop listening to your brain, but rather hear all the voices, and feel the emotions. Use the logic and intuition in balance to overcome self-doubt.

**Fall in love with your true self:**

Loving yourself is anything but narcissistic. If you don't become your best friend, who else will? If you don't convey confidence in what you do, don't expect others to trust you.

## Forming a Strong Sense of Self

**Self-Confidence:**

Confidence is the stuff that turns thoughts into actions.

**Self-Esteem:**

You believe you are worthy of love and respect, and you hold a generally positive perception of yourself.

**Self-Compassion:**
We give ourselves the same kindness and care we give our good friends.

**Optimism:**
This is a state of mind in which someone is hopeful about what will happen in the future. Optimistic people expect the best possible outcome, not the worst.

**Break the habit:**
At the end of the day, self-doubt is a habit, nothing more, nothing less.

And regardless of where it came from, you can work to free yourself from chronic self-doubt by building better habits.

## Logical Approach

The information above is the modern, logical, psychological, masculine approach to over coming self-doubt, which is only one half of the story.

## Spiritual Approach

What this book is about is the spiritual Divine Feminine approach to overcoming self-doubt, the other half of the story where the root to our self-doubts actually comes from.

My training in holistic nutrition taught me not to just treat a symptom. For a cure you have to reverse engineer and get to the root of the problem. Thus far we have been addressing the symptoms of self-doubt. Going forward we are going to dig deep and get to the root of our self doubt.

My intent is for you to have a spiritual awakening to your true self and purpose which will wipe away any lies you have believed and self doubts you have bought into.

A spiritual awakening may happen all at once by learning information that will instantly change your life forever or it may happen little by little over time.

When we undergo a spiritual awakening, we literally "wake up" to a feeling of more possibilities for our life. We may feel like we have outgrown our current life. We begin to question our old beliefs, habits, and social conditioning, and see that there is much more to life than what we have been taught or allowed to experience.

You are more powerful than you have been allowed to believe. Your Divinity, your specialness, your femaleness, and your self worth, once revealed will wipe away any self doubt you ever had about yourself. You will be fearless and never feel you have to bow down to anyone or feel second rate to anyone again.

# CHAPTER 2

## Spiritual Awakening

*A Divine Feminine is a spiritual seeker,*
*always asking the deep questions.*

Once upon a time all of us were indigenous. At some point in the past we all had ancestors who came from a very particular place, a land where our grandmothers' stories lived.

A woman who knows her ancient history is powerful, she knows she is the descendant of sacred grandmothers. This knowledge can be a powerful tool for understanding and healing a person's circumstances and problems.

The experiences of your ancestral lineage have created a storehouse of information and potential. Much of this potential lies dormant in the subconscious mind, covered by cultural expectations, social norms, and religious programming.

Women are beginning to remember who they are, who they were in the beginning of history and who they want to be in the future. Their Divine Feminine Energy is being awakened. Women are organizing support groups and rallying together and supporting each other rather than competing against each other.

Historically, male dominance has tried to tame us and patriarchal societies have tried to control us. We are not meant to be property, abused, dominated or controlled.

Women today are on a tremendous spiritual search. About 80% of participants at transformational centers, continuing education classes, retreats and spiritual centers are women. Behind this surging feminine energy is a yearning to understand who they are and what their true purpose in life is. Women often feel that, along with a portion of their history, they're missing a part of themselves.

- Do you ever find yourself questioning the beliefs handed down to you from your family and community?
- Do you feel restless and dissatisfied with your life?
- Do you find yourself asking deep questions?
- Do you feel unfulfilled in your current role in life?
- Are you looking for a way out of your current situation?
- Do you feel like you don't fit in?
- Do you feel your potential is passing you by?
- Are you wanting to leave a relationship, job or religion?
- Are you trying to fit yourself into a life that doesn't feel authentic to you?
- Are you looking for a new tribe? A new way of life? A new you?

These feelings are the beginning of the "awakening" that is happening across the whole world. Women are waking up to their divinity and a knowing that they are here on earth for more, capable of more, and desire more than the limitations placed on them.

A spiritual awakening is not usually pleasant. Often it feels like confusion, frustration, anger, sadness, grief and being out of place. A spiritual awakening can be uncomfortable and challenging because it is an intense time of growth as you are evolving.

We are living in an exciting time of history when the energies are changing and people are changing. We are becoming more aware that we are more than our physical bodies and there is more to life than working, acquiring worldly goods and paying bills. We have a longing to be more and find our purpose in life and reason for being on earth. We feel a need to contribute to the betterment of the world. This is part of the awakening we hear so much about.

- Awakening is becoming aware of the limitations that we have been living under
- Awakening is having a "knowing" that you have a spiritual purpose for being on earth at this time
- Awakening is throwing off the shackles of historical patriarchal control
- Awakening is feeling the power of your femaleness and divinity
- Awakening is feeling deeper about everything

## So, why do spiritual awakenings happen in the first place?

Spiritual awakenings happen as a natural product of your Soul evolving, expanding, and maturing. Just as everything in life grows, so too does our connection with our Souls.

Before we came to earth we made an agreement with our heavenly parents about what our mission was and what we wanted to accomplish with our lives on earth. Our spiritual awakening is the heavens whispering to us, to wake us up and help us remember our purpose.

When you are unhappy in a situation, don't stay in denial and try to make it work out. Your soul knows there are better plans for you, trust in the process. Trust in yourself and your intuition. Calm your mind and look deep within. It is through this place that you can access your intuition and live a more inspired and spiritually guided life, while enjoying the peace, support and synchronicities that come with doing so.

Never discredit your gut instinct. You are not paranoid or crazy. Your body can pick up on bad vibrations. If something deep inside of you says something is not right about a person or situation, trust it.

Remember, inner guidance is subtle, so don't strain to hear messages. Just trust that you have received the information at a deeper level by the simple yet profound act of connecting with your Spirit and any answers you need will arise as you are ready. In the meantime, enjoy the peace and stillness within.

Connecting with this part of yourself is the beginning of your awakening. It requires a constant and consistent practice of becoming present and turning your attention inward and not worrying about what others may think, or feeling like you have to explain yourself.

Pay attention to whatever inspires you, for it is Spirit trying to communicate with you. That is why it is called "inspiration" as in-spirit. Listen to it, believe it and act on it.

With the past and future swirling around us now, we are given a brief glimpse into our soul's intended purpose. The Goddess energy within us is struggling to be recognized and utilized in the quest to bring back the Divine Feminine Energy and spiritual balance into our broken world.

We were born with the seeds of gods and goddesses inside us. When we awaken to our divinity we can release shame-based belief systems and their limitations. We can no longer deny that there is a universal ripple effect of the Divine Feminine waking up in the world. The rise of the Divine Feminine within us will help heal our self-doubts and past limitations.

# CHAPTER 3

## What is Divine Feminine Energy?

> *"The future of the world depends on the full restoration of the Sacred Feminine in all its tenderness, passion, divine ferocity, and surrendered persistence".* **Andrew Harvey**

For several years there has been talk and interest in "Divine Feminine Energy" believed to be very strong on earth at this time. Women today are on a tremendous spiritual search. Behind this restless surging feminine energy is a yearning to understand who they are and what their purpose in life is.

Our mothers couldn't teach us what they didn't know about the lost power of the Divine Feminine or how to truly embrace ourselves. The patriarchal societies value masculine energy traits such as achievement, warrior spirit and linear thinking. This may leave us, as women, successful in the workplace but broken down and burned out in the rest of our lives; yearning for a balance, for a sacred feminine that we barely remember exists.

The feminist movements of the last century have allowed women to vote, get an education and enter the work force in just about any position they desire. Women still struggle for equal pay and being treated with respect by male coworkers. Women are still expected to be wives and mothers, running a household taking care of meals, laundry, schedules, etc. They suffer from guilt if they choose a career over having a family. They suffer from resentment if they begrudgingly choose a family and forgo the career. And when they try to have both they find it difficult to be happy and successful at everything. The stress makes it easy to fall into depression and substance abuse. The problem is that women are trying to be "equal" to men by taking on masculine energy, and being the same as men to cope in a masculine world.

Since the feminist movement in the 60's women have been trying to take back their power by demasculinizing men to diminish their power. It comes from an understandable place. We have felt powerless to men for a few thousand years so it was natural to come from a place of anger and revenge.

Today women and men are locked in a power struggle against each other. Men try to take power from women only to find they are not attracted to or respect weak, co-dependent women. Women try to take power back from men only to realize they are not attracted to or respect demasculinized, confused over grown children. We are not attracted to weakness in each other.

Acting like a man, talking like a man, thinking like a man, dressing like a man, doing as a man does, and taking power from a man is not working. So now what?

## Striving To Be Equal to Men Was Misguided

For thousands of years, we have been collectively and individually tapped into our masculine energy, to the extreme. We have allowed it to dominate our own existence, which has influenced the way the human race responds to life. As a result of not being true to our Divine Feminine selves, life is lopsided and completely out of balance.

Just look at the world's systems. We have lived in a patriarchal world. Religious organizations are mostly organized by men. God is referred to as "Him." Men have dominated politics and leadership. Most CEOs and business owners are men. Finally, at this stage of our evolution, humanity is recognizing the value of the Divine Feminine and shifting towards a new world view.

All over the world, we are bearing witness to the Divine Feminine materializing. Now more than ever, women are coming together to tear down an antiquated system that only honors masculine energy. Women manage businesses, pursue careers, run countries and achieve their dreams, all while raising children and taking care of communities.

Men are not inferior to women, they are different. They have their own sacred purpose and journey on this earth. Unfortunately their history for a few thousand years has been one of violence and false belief they have the right to have domination over the earth and other human beings, without being accountable for their cruelty. But they too are beginning to wake up to their sacred selves.

In the meantime, as we strive to reach our divine feminine full potential, our goal is not to mimic male energy and compete with men. We don't need to. We are the Divine Feminine and we have our own ways.

Realistically, and ironically, true femininity is strong. A woman can be soft and strong, tender and tough, deferring and dignified, all at the same time.

The pursuit of equality has robbed us of more than it gave. With all the early feminists slogans I heard growing up; "hear me roar", "clawing our way up the corporate ladder", "breaking the glass ceiling", proving that "anything you can do I can do better", "to all the men who want to hold us down" and "Down with the Man!", we've become hard, tough, independent women, and in our own delusion, we applaud ourselves for these qualities instead of mourning the death of our naturally-powerful Divine Feminine attributes.

Equal doesn't have to be the same. That's where we got sorely misguided. To become more like men doesn't make us equal. We were already equal but vastly different. That difference is incredible! Femininity is a unique gift. Our softness and all that it encapsulates is a powerful force and it is a strength we already possess and don't have to fight for.

## Evolution of the Divine Feminine

The power we've been mastering for the last 100 years has been the masculine version of power. Until now, power has been defined exclusively in masculine terms. If you look up the word "power" in the dictionary, the definition given is the ability "to do, to act, to accomplish, to wield command or control over others."

This masculine power system has given us the miracles of science and the marvels of industry. It has enabled us to create an unprecedented standard of living and opportunities beyond our great-grandmothers' wildest dreams. Conversely, our "comforts" have made our lives so easy we have become lazy, sickly, weak minded and disconnected from the natural world.

It was a brilliant strategy for women to collectively take on mastering the masculine power system, to level the playing field between men and women and emancipate ourselves from the tyranny of oppression.

Though there is still a long way to go, especially on a global scale, we have become the most autonomous, free, independent, educated, and powerful generation of women. In fact, the yearnings we have for self-expression, spiritual partnership, creativity and contribution are high quality problems we're now navigating as a result of our unprecedented success at mastering power in the masculine.

It's an odd paradox that the kind of power that has brought us to this point is not the power that we now need to move forward. Indeed, if we look at what's missing from our lives and from our world, we can see that the things we most deeply desire, such as:

- love
- intimacy
- connection
- belonging
- creativity
- self-expression
- aliveness
- meaning
- purpose
- contribution
- a brighter future for generations to come

None of which can be created with a system of masculine power based on control, analysis, and logical, linear thinking. Nor can they be executed with a strategic plan.

While many people are speaking about a return of the feminine, it is both a return and an evolution of the feminine that holds the key to our personal power and planetary transformation. The feminine of our recent and ancient past, however healing and nourishing, is insufficient to empower us to create those things that are critical for our personal and collective future. For the feminine to become a source of power from which we can create the future of our lives and the future of our world, it needs to be consciously evolved through us.

The return of Divine Feminine Energy is not about

overpowering men or taking control and switching over to a matriarchal society from a patriarchal society.

We need to awaken and cultivate a new, co-creative, feminine power that integrates and includes all the gains of masculine power, giving us access to a kind of co-creativity we've never seen in our recorded history.

When both sexes rise to their divine power, one cannot triumph over the other. There will be balance, hope, wisdom, and the unique gifts that both men and women share with one another and with the world. Only then will there be change, equality, respect, cooperation and peace on earth.

## What Exactly is Divine Feminine Energy?

Remember, we are talking about the spiritual aspect of what it means to be human, divine and feminine.

Divine has many definitions, but the one that stands out is: "supremely good, heavenly, Godlike". Feminine also has several definitions, but this one seems the most appropriate: "the embodiment or conception of a timeless or idealized feminine nature."

Just as all humans share the same hormones, males and females have different balances of those hormones. Example: Males have more testosterone, making them more aggressive (naturally good protectors) and sexually active (to repopulate and continue the human species on earth).

Females have more estrogen allowing them to create life and feel emotions deep enough to fiercely protect her children.

Males and females also share the same divine energies in different balances. Unlike hormones which we don't have control over, with thought and intention we do have control over how we choose to use and cultivate our divine energies.

The feminine is intuitive, wise, and loving. The main aspects of the divine feminine are:

- sensuality
- creativity
- fertility
- compassion
- empathy
- love
- receptivity
- acceptance
- restoration
- life
- renewal
- creation
- birth
- healing
- openness
- motherhood
- nurturing
- love
- understanding
- compassion
- insight
- forgiveness
- the moon
- connection
- harmony

If a man or woman does not properly channel their femininity, they can become co-dependent, overly emotional, irrational, sacrificial to one's own detriment, disorganized, confused, and lost. This results in dysfunctional relationships, mental health issues like bipolar disorder, a constant feeling of burnout, a lack of productivity, a loss of self-worth, a "damsel in distress mentality," and the inability to complete projects.

When expressed in its truest form, this energy goes with the flow, births new possibilities and ideas through creativity, promotes unconditional love, has beautiful and nurturing relationships, and provides a safe space for those who need to feel protected.

Here are a few qualities of the Divine Masculine: logical, left-brained, action oriented toward an end goal, physical strength, the use of brute force, seeks self-mastery, introspective, closed off, protective, provides, competitive, firm, in constant motion, has a need to "do", seeks material possessions as a marker of success, concerned with order, makes decisions based on information, focused on the physical world and appearances.

This is just a short list. Keep in mind that the Divine Masculine can get out of harmony. When it does, these characteristics go to an extreme end of the spectrum. If a man or woman does not properly channel their masculinity, they can become controlling, overbearing, unemotional, achieve much but love too little, materialistic, egotistical, and obsessed with looks. This results in greed, corruption, war, materialism, and abuse of power.

When the Divine Masculine is expressed in its purest form, it is strong but gentle, kind, protective, loving, goal-oriented, successful, generous, spiritual, and hard-working.

While these two energies do coexist within the same person, they are opposing energies, which have been designed to work together to create harmony and balance.

The Divine Feminine and Masculine energies transcend gender. Every man has feminine energy, although most are out of touch with it because they have been shamed into believing this is a sign of weakness or homosexuality.

Likewise, every woman has masculine energy. However; unlike a man's instinct to suppress their femininity, most of us are quite comfortable with the masculine aspect of ourselves. After all, we have relied heavily upon it to survive in a "man's world".

Unfortunately, many of us have neglected our own femininity in the name of success and survival. For us as women, some of those reasons have been that we've thought our feminine aspects would make us appear weak in a man's world. That we wouldn't be taken seriously. That we wouldn't get ahead at best, or keep our jobs, at worst. That we'd be laughed at, ignored, rejected. That we simply would not survive.

## Time To Soften

It's time to change that. It's time to soften. It's time to reclaim our beautiful Divine Feminine qualities, to bring them into balance with our masculine ones, and to own all parts of ourselves. I'm talking about our empathy, our intuition, our kindness, vulnerability, creativity, nurturing of ourselves and others, our inner wisdom and knowing, and our big beautiful hearts.

There is a rising that is taking place amongst women all around the world. A rising to take back what is ours. To redefine our womanhood. To value once again the core essence of who we are. It's a reckoning. A reclamation. A revolution even.

In order for harmony to be restored to the world, we must tap into the Divine Feminine side of human nature. We don't need to throw out our masculine traits. We need those traits to take our place in the world, to lead. But we need to bring those masculine traits into balance with the lost feminine.

## Lead Like Women

To reshape the world, we need to lead like women, not be bad clones of men, and our feminine traits are the pathway home. To be able to balance our ability to listen and nurture with our ability to drive and control. To be able to lead with authority, and at the same time show our vulnerability. To care for our people as much as we care about profits.

There are many influential women and potentially influential women in the public eye at this time. Unfortunately too many of them are still locked into the masculine energy version of power and authority and it is abrasive and off-putting to many. We have passed the time when women need to act like men to gain respect. If they would soften their edges a little and not be afraid to lead with Divine Feminine Energy they would be much more effective in delivering their messages and influencing many more individuals.

## Feminine is the New Balance

*"Everything you need, your courage,*
*strength, compassion and love; everything*
*you need is already within you."*

The New Divine Feminine is modern woman's way of connecting to ancient ways of being a woman. Feminine Energy is what the world needs; compassion, acceptance, healing, nurturing, love, understanding and creativity.

Become who you were born to be; a woman who owns and honors all parts of herself. A woman who realizes the profound power that is inside of her and is not afraid to live, love and work as the Divine Feminine she is. A woman who knows how to be strong and feminine at the same time.

# CHAPTER 4

## Herstory Our Ancient Spiritual Heritage

Many women believe that women's real history has been disguised and distorted when history was rewritten by male Victors and male historians and therefore have been dispossessed of a heritage, tradition and sense of identity that was once uniquely their own.

## Historians

History is always written by those in power. Historians have erased and changed bits of social and religious history to serve their purposes and world views at the time. Historians have traditionally been male, skewed with a male perspective.

Her-story is the history of women by women vs history (his-story) written by men with a male bias. As women historians entered the field in record numbers, they brought with them new questions, developed new methods, and sought for evidence of women's presence in neglected texts and exciting new findings. Many history books have now been written from a female perspective.

History colors our comprehension of the world and our place in it. It filters our perceptions of reality. It defines what is acceptable and what is not. It shapes our sense of self. Restoring our history of goddess-based societies that functioned peacefully for centuries in accordance with more democratic spiritual beliefs than those now in existence helps women and men to cut through oppressive and destructive cultural stereotypes of today.

## In the Beginning When Women Were Revered

The first people on earth in prehistory that we have discovered are the Paleolithic indigenous tribes all over the world; Europe, Asia, Africa, India, China, Iran, Egypt, Turkey, Australia, Russia, Greece, Italy, Spain, Canada, North and South America, etc. These humans lived on earth before written language existed, but they left behind other kinds of remains and artifacts which tell us about their lives. They were the first humans known to have created works of art, to include sculpture carvings and cave drawings, which appear to be an intentional record of spiritual concepts, accumulated information and acquired wisdom.

Prehistory is the Paleolithic period also known as the Stone Age, the earliest period of human development and the longest phase of mankind's history. Hollywood and cartoons have led us to believe these humans were more ape-like and less intelligent than modern man, but that isn't so. Science and archeology have now disproved Darwin's theory of evolution and know that we showed up on earth 200,000 years ago, with the same bodies, minds and DNA as we currently have. There was no evolution involved and we have not changed or evolved into anything else since that time.

In the earliest of times these people lived in small groups or tribes which had very similar cultures and spiritual beliefs without ever having any contact with each other.

Each tribe had a shaman who was responsible for the community's health, physical, mental and spiritual needs. They performed sacred rites and ceremonies, led pilgrimages and festivals, they played drums and rattles for meditation and dancing, chanting and singing. A shaman's life belonged to the village and it was their responsibility to ensure the peoples well-being. The shaman was the most important person in each tribe or community. Shamans were respected and paid for their work in food, hides, and other items of value.

The shaman was an intermediary between this world and the spirit world. They acted on behalf of the community and retrieved information from spirit helpers for healing, hunting, finding food and resolution of community quarrels, etc.

The earliest spiritual beliefs were; there is a spirit world, life after death, and spirit guides and helpers who are eager to guide us on our earthly journey. The shaman could enter the spirit world while in a deep trance or meditation. Unlike Buddhist monks and yogic practitioners who practice for years to reach this state of meditation, the shaman uses the monotonous beat of a drum or rattle to reach the deep theta state required for deep meditation where one receives visions, enlightenment, epiphanies and "a knowing" to the questions they are searching for.

The first shamans were women or gay men. Today, even though most indigenous shamans are men, the shaman's traditional ceremonial clothing still looks like women's clothing.

## Ancient Women's Place in Society

Women held high and important positions throughout early history, they were shamans, healers, prophetesses, priestesses, Queens, Temple accountants, money lenders and real estate holders. Temple priestesses developed the first written language and the first calendars.

Women seemed to hold the most prominent positions in the social and religious structure of the community. The sleeping platforms of the women of the household were always built into the east wall of the living quarters and were raised slightly higher than the men's, whose quarters seem to shift in location from household to household.

Once a woman passed out of the cycle of bleeding and giving birth, her blood was considered "wise blood" and its energy flowed in the guise of prophecy. Oracles prophesied at temples and shrines all over the Mediterranean. In the ancient world, no one, made important decisions without consulting oracles. Oracles were almost always women past the age of childbirth. The older women were honored and respected for their wisdom and grandmothers traditionally had the role of guiding the tribe and the young.

## Sex in the Ancient World

In the oldest of times women's bodies were considered holy, because they had the seemingly magical ability to give birth, to create new human beings and nourish them with the fluids from their breasts. Because new life came from women's bodies as it did from the earth, women were celebrated as an embodiment of the divine.

Most all of the ancient Goddess statues have very large breasts, as if full of milk, some have large pregnant stomachs and there are many symbols of the vulva and reproductive systems, to depict the sacredness of the divine feminine woman.

The ancients viewed the act of sex as a sacred union. The divine experience of sexual ecstasy and orgasm was a metaphor for the release of healing spiritual, psychological, and physical energy.

The indigenous cultures and later the Egyptians did not view nudity as shameful. Bodies were beautiful and who they were. Sex and sexuality was beautiful, sacred and normal. It wasn't until Christianity took over and imposed their moral views on society that nudity was no longer acceptable.

The current view of morality makes it difficult for many historians and clergy to understand sexuality as an expression of divinity. As a result, sexual priestesses in Temples were labeled prostitutes, concubines and courtesans; insulting words that misrepresent the sanctity of an ancient rite.

## Female Deities

Due to the technological advances in the field of archaeology, a wealth of new information about prehistory has come to light. Stone Age markings once dismissed as meaningless are being reinterpreted as the earliest evidence of spiritual symbolism. Thousands of images of an ancient Great Goddess and her mythologies have been excavated. Relics of the societies that revered her and sacred sites where they worshiped, bear witness to a history of Goddess worship that has been forgotten and buried.

In prehistoric times spirituality was founded on the worship of female deities. Great Goddess, who evolved into many goddesses around the world were worshiped as the Divine Mother. The Goddess and those who performed her sacred rituals were female and appear in some of the earliest representations of spiritual rituals.

The Great Goddess was not the female version of the Christian God the Father. She did not rule the world. She was the world. She was the personification of the reproductive energies of nature, birth, death, fertility and motherhood. She was the Great Mother, Divine Feminine, Gaia, Pachamama, the earth, the seas, the seasons. She was a healer and destroyer. She was the maiden, mother, mage and crone. She was the protector and warrior. She was the sacred. She was life.

In the ancient matriarchal view, retrievable from myths and legends, although in each culture this Goddess had a different name, she seems to be the same deity. The Goddesses were regarded as the sole origin of orderly, logical thought. Out of her intellectual gifts to women arose such disciplines as mathematics (originally meaning "mother-wisdom"), calendars (originally "lunar" or "menstrual"), systems of measurement, musical and poetic forms, architectural techniques, and many other formal procedures for dealing with both art and nature.

For several thousands of years, this nurturing Divine Feminine represented the ultimate spiritual example enabling women and men to understand who they were, within themselves and in relation to their families, communities, and environment. They lived in peace and flourished and did not engage in warfare. Skeletal remains reveal that at least three distinct racial types harmoniously coexisted.

Traces of societies in the middle Paleolithic period of time, when climate change and rising seas forced them to move and group together in larger communities, based their spiritual structures around a goddess. They lived in peace, with role models for the sexes very different from those now of the norm. It is believed that their religion was created and conducted by priestesses. Their hierarchical order of importance in the divine family was "mother, daughter, son and father."

From the dawn of prehistory, women were perceived as holy, sacred, and divine incarnations of the Great Mother Goddess. Powerful figures full of strength, wisdom, and leadership, women were the keepers of the human race, from which all life flowed.

In her book When God Was a Woman, Merlin Stone writes: "In prehistoric and historic periods of human development, religions existed in which people revered their supreme creator as female. The Great Goddess, the Divine Ancestress, had been worshiped from the beginnings of the Neolithic periods of 7000 BC until the closing of the last Goddess temples, about AD 500." She also writes: "Archaeological, mythological and historical evidence all reveal that the female religion, far from naturally fading away, was the victim of centuries of continual persecution and suppression by the advocates of the newer religions which held male deities as supreme."

## Ancient Women

From the first humans on earth women were revered as creators of life, healers, spiritual guides, shamans and the leaders of tribes. Under their guidance there was no war, slavery or conquering other tribes. They lived in peace for thousands of years.

Women and Goddesses are universally credited with the invention of agriculture, they are seen as the originators of many other civilized pursuits; shelters, the manufacture of clothing, pottery, utensils, and tools; the domestication of animals, the development of decorative arts, music, alphabets, numbers, calendars, and other systems of calculation and record keeping.

In the earliest times, old tribal mothers were credited with the important religious or magical lore, including the knowledge of right and wrong that led them to formulate laws and other rules of behavior. As mothers made the rules for their children's safety, and socialization, so the ancient tribal mothers made the rules to guide the behavior of all. One reason for its success may well be that the laws were made chiefly by women, whose quicker awareness of connections and relationships would have made them fairer lawmakers than men. The laws were largely benevolent and pacifist, foreshadowing the "golden rule". Some of the laws commanded that no one should cause pain to others, nor make anyone sorrowful, nor steal, cheat, bear false witness, stir up strife; neither should anyone harm animals, damage fertile land, or befoul waters.

As the indigenous tribes were conquered and assimilated into male dominated and Christian cultures, their history, ceremonies and spiritual rites were forbidden and eventually forgotten. The stories and teaching that had been verbally handed down from one generation to the next were no longer told.

It hasn't been until recent years that archaeologists and science has advanced enough that they have been able to unearth and re-look at ancient artifacts, cave drawings and DNA testing to put the pieces together of what our ancient ancestors' daily lives were like, their spirituality, healing and relationships.

To their surprise they found that it was the women, not the men who were the first leaders of the world.

These are our roots, we modern contemporary women, all of us, are reflections and descendants of the ancient Divine Feminine, the Eternal Goddess.

## Invasions and Violence

Around five thousand years ago, a new power doomed the goddess to eventual oblivion.

Indo-European nomads referred to as either Kurgans or Aryans, rode horse-drawn chariots and brandished swords as they violently invaded and conquered peaceful villages. Aryan war tactics included massacre and rape. They attempted to impose their cultural values on their victims in a similar fashion. They believed they had the "rightful domain" over nature, animals, and womankind.

The peaceful non-warring goddess-based cultures were no match for the invaders who imposed their fiercely patriarchal, male dominance, male violence and male authoritarian social system on the indigenous tribes they conquered. Gradually the symbols of the goddesses were demonized and imbued with evil connotations. The shift from female religious authority to male military power relegated women to the status of property. By stripping women of their power, their purpose was solely for man's pleasure and to bear his children, preferably males.

# Christianity

There was a Christian community in Rome as early as A.D. 57. Initially in Rome, Christianity was the religion of foreigners. It appealed to the poor, immigrants and slaves. Christianity was the only religion without social, race, financial, or educational barriers. And women were encouraged to bear large numbers of children to increase the ranks of the Christians. Not surprisingly, the sect grew rapidly from generation to generation.

Roman church fathers used their growing political and military power to eradicate all traces of the Great Goddess. They insisted on the exclusive worship of one male deity, served by an all-male priesthood. Women were not allowed to speak in church or attend funerals. Henceforth divinity was to be exclusively masculine. The suppression of women was directly linked to the suppression of the Goddess.

The Christians were ruthless in their determination to destroy the indigenous people who would not convert to Christianity and forsake their Goddess worship. Temples were systematically destroyed and key ceremonies were outlawed.

Originally pagan meant "the people who are here" as referred to by the Christians, who were at that time considered the foreigners. A Pagan was anyone who worshiped gods that were different to those worshiped by the Romans and the Greeks.

The original pagans were followers of an ancient religion that worshiped several gods. They were demonized, driven out and killed by the Christians who also destroyed their Temples, Learning Centers, Libraries, and Universities, in their determination to destroy all traces of pre-Christian civilization.

Christian doctrine eventually succeeded in robbing women of their spiritual heritage. The powerful churchmen of the Christian church had great influence over the minds of the populace. The churchmen would interpret the scriptures and only they could determine if you could be forgiven of your sins or excommunicated and doomed to damnation.

Christian men slaughtered their enemies in unending wars, crusades and persecutions, while their church was the richest institution in Europe and the main population lived in abject poverty. Women were the poorest of all under Christian laws that allowed them to own nothing, not even their own clothing.

## Religion's Control

By the Middle Ages reality was being defined by the powerful churchmen of the Christian church. They were creating a reality which places their idea of God's plan for mankind at the very center of life, which was, that life is a spiritual test for one solitary purpose; to win or lose salvation. And in this test you must correctly choose between two opposing forces: the force of God or the temptations of the devil. But you didn't face this challenge alone, in fact you weren't qualified, you needed the churchmen to guide you every step of the way. The churchmen would interpret the scriptures, tell you if you were living in accordance to God's will or being duped by the devil and only they determined if you could be forgiven of your sins. If you followed their instructions you were assured a rewarding afterlife, and if you didn't there was excommunication and you would surely be doomed to damnation. The people completely believed the churchmen.

In many societies, religion has often been used to explain things such as social inequality (some families have been chosen by God to rule; some people were chosen by God to be slaves) and the social superiority of men.

Thus, in many societies, religious teachings emphasize the "naturalness" and "sacred nature" of the patriarchy in which men are viewed as superior to women; men are more important than women; men are to be "breadwinners" while women are supposed to be mothers, "housewives," and breeding machines. The social roles of men and women, according to religious teachings, are not only sacred truths but many people believe that they are scientific facts. Many religions emphasize or reinforce the idea of patriarchy as natural, as given to humans by a deity, and therefore women are to be subject to rule, domination, and ownership by men.

With regard to Islam, Karen Armstrong, in her book Islam: A Short History, writes: "The women of the first ummah in Medina took full part in its public life, and some, according to Arab custom, fought alongside the men in battle. They did not seem to have experienced Islam as an oppressive religion, though later, as happened in Christianity, men would hijack the faith and bring it into line with the prevailing patriarchy."

## Scripture Edits

Scriptures hinting at feminine primacy or power were eliminated from the canon (a collection of books written by apostles and those close to an apostle which the church chose and approved as the word of God and considered scripture. Eventually to become the Old and New Testaments. There were many more books and documents not included in the canon, especially those pertaining to women.), and later male scholars tended to overlook the few remaining allusions to an early matriarchate, such as the period when women "judged" all Israel (Judg. 4), or the statement that the owners of houses were mothers, not fathers (Ruth 1:8). Sometimes the words translated as "God" in the English Bible were actually feminine plurals in the original language, or the Hebrew plural elohim, meaning not "God" but goddesses and gods.

Similarly, the word saga has been translated out of its original meaning, "she who speaks". The original meaning of saga was "female sage".

Eve is called ezer, the Hebrew word for "help", in Genesis 2:18. This same word was used to describe God as a divine help in Deuteronomy 33:7, 26, 29; Psalm 33:20; 70:5; 115:9-11; and 146:5. Because the same word was used to describe God, it cannot imply that Eve was inferior to Adam.

Many obscure words bear witness to male scholars tendency to stretch translations into patriarchal favor. Every variety of ancient Christianity that advocated the legitimacy of women's leadership was eventually declared heretical, and evidence of women's early leadership roles was erased or suppressed.

This erasure has taken many forms. Collections of prophetic oracles were destroyed. Texts were changed. For example, at least one woman's place in history was obscured by turning her into a man! Concluding that women could not be apostles, textual editors and translators transformed Junia into Junias, a man. Romans 16:7

The Bible itself was named after Byblos, one of the Great Mother's oldest cities, where her priestesses kept a great library of papyrus scrolls that the Greeks called byblos (bibles)

Gnostic scriptures suggested that the feminine principle of wisdom was embodied in Eve, whom the Bible called Mother of All Living. As in the Gorgon symbol, Eve's feminine wisdom was linked to the serpent who taught man the all important knowledge of good and evil, without which he could never hope to achieve heaven. Some Gnostics revered the serpent and Eve as the liberators of humanity.

Obviously, Gnostic scriptures had a different slant on the creation story from the one that became canonical, which left out the female principle and demonized her serpent. Orthodox Christians collected and burned many copies of the two or three hundred different alternative gospels in the fourth and fifth centuries. New found texts that survived are therefore crucial in constructing a fuller and more accurate portrait. The Gospel of Mary, for example, argued that leadership should be based on spiritual maturity, regardless of whether one is male or female. This Gospel lets us hear an alternative voice to the one dominant in canonized works like I Timothy, which tried to silence women and insist that their salvation lies in bearing children. Where references to the Goddess couldn't be demonized, masculinized, or quietly dropped, early churchmen tended to convert them into mythical saints. Since Europeans persisted in attending the same old pagan shrines, often the church's only recourse was to canonize the local native deity as a long-ago martyr, and supply relics to replace the ancient idol.

When Goddess worshiping ceremonies persisted among medieval Europeans, churches often tolerated or even supported them, after inventing a new legend to provide Christianized rationale. Many pagan customs survived as spring processionals, Maypole dances, solstitial bonfires, harvest homes, well dressings, carnival games, and other remnants of the ancient sacred drama.

The formal elimination of women from official roles of leadership did not eliminate women's actual presence and importance to the Christian tradition, although it certainly seriously damaged their capacity to contribute fully. What is remarkable is how much evidence has survived systematic attempts to erase women from history, and with them the warrants and models for women's leadership. The evidence presented here is but the tip of an iceberg.

## The Burning Times - Convert or Die

Early Christianity began to grow and spread fear across the world in many different lands. While the average person was living their normal lives, their cultures were full of what is believed to be gods and goddesses, superstitions, rituals, healers, cunning folk, medicine men and women, spiritual leaders, and many other titles in the various communities, tribes, and clans.

As Christianity evolved, they realized that the old ways of the people were very ingrained in their lives. If Christianity was going to take root, they would have to distort the beliefs and practices of the peoples and absorb the cultural beliefs.

Gods and Goddesses were either demonized or turned into Saints in order to capture the hearts of the people. The people in the cities were converted first and it took greater efforts to convert the country dweller or those living in the rural areas of societies. The small rural towns just didn't seem to want to convert. This was a big concern of the early Christian leaders.

This Christian religion converted leaders of Kingdoms or governments because back then there were no constitutions to separate church and state. As Christianity moved across the lands, they realized that the people were not easily accepting the new beliefs, with the new taxes and the new requirements.

The healers, spiritual leaders, cunning folk became a threat and so the Christians called them witches and their practices witchcraft. Many of these condemned witches were herbalists, alchemists, astrologists, midwives, or just old. It was a dark time in history. It was the medieval times when torture was commonly practiced and was an expectation in society life. A dark time when threats of death were constant and fear of the rulers and the leaders of Christianity was growing.

It was a time when people were being tortured and burned as heretics for not converting and accepting the new religion. Disagreeing with the church was a crime of heresy and was punishable by death. There are reports of whole towns being murdered. Whole towns were wiped out of women and young female children. Although, men who stood up for these women and any children and even their pets were often murdered and it was common to be burned at the stake, although the torture was not limited to being burned. To burn in this world was to condemn the victim to the eternal lake of fire in Hell.

## Shamans

The Shamanic practices of many cultures were virtually wiped out with the spread of Christianity. Beginning with the middle ages and continuing to the Renaissance, remnants of European shamanism were wiped out by campaigns against witches. The campaigns were often orchestrated by the Catholic Inquisition.

The repression of shamanism continued as Christian influence spread with Spanish colonization. In the Caribbean, and Central and South America, Catholic priests followed the footsteps of the Conquistadors and were instrumental in the destruction of the local traditions, ignorantly denouncing practitioners as "devil worshipers" and having them executed. In North America, the English Puritans conducted periodic campaigns against individuals perceived as witches. As recently as the 1970s, historic petroglyphs were being defaced by missionaries in the Amazon.

## Colonialism

When the first English-speaking colonists began their invasion of North America, they described Native Americans as "living by the hunt" in spite of the fact Native Americans were farmers whose surplus agricultural products fed the first English colonists. The problem was that Indian women were the farmers and owned the fields and the produce. To those who viewed the world through patriarchal eyes, the work of women didn't count and hence it was important to create the hunting myth to reinforce men's economic contributions.

Under the patriarchy, men control women's bodies. Thus the first Europeans were shocked by the fact that Indian women controlled their own bodies and could freely express their sexuality.

Under the patriarchy, men owned their wives and the children they produced. This was expressed, and continues to be expressed, in having the wives and their children use the man's surname. The Europeans had a difficult time understanding that in many American Indian cultures, women could freely divorce their husbands, that they could have more than one husband at a time, and that their children belonged to the mother's family rather than to the father's family.

Rather than see the numerous American Indian examples which surrounded them as evidence that patriarchy wasn't "natural," the Europeans simply forced patriarchy and Christianity upon the Indians.

# CHAPTER 5

## Consequences Of the Suppression Of the Divine Feminine

Once, women were honored as strong, beautiful, creative, sensual beings. The feminine aspect of life was necessary for our very survival, and the sacred feminine was honored by ancients around the world as the bringers of life. Woman was life itself. The power of women in those ancient times was undeniable, without women, we humans would not be here now.

As male dominance succeeded in stripping women of their power and spiritual heritage, civilizations also lost their connection to Mother Earth. Skills women possessed, once considered sacred, have been turned over to industry, mass production, and big business. It was the shift to ownership of crop and land (usually by an elite class of landholders and the Church) that spelled the end of the goddess and her gift economy. In order for the new capitalistic order to succeed, women's role in food production and their spiritual authority had to be removed. Women's traditional access to land, and control over the crops they cultivated was replaced by a labor force.

Today in the Western world we are still living with the consequences of the destruction of the Goddess cultures and limiting a woman's capacity to envision her own full potential as a human being. Cultures driven by this belief system have contributed to the inequities and violence that women continue to struggle against every day.

We may live in the twenty-first century, but eighteenth century patriarchal ideas about women's roles are still embedded in our minds, and church leaders misinterpret the Bible to defend this view. Gender bias is still entrenched in organized religions around the world.

From the very beginning of the Christian Era cultural prejudice against women has been allowed to prevail. In the middle ages pastors used the bible to defend wife beating. During the Inquisition both Catholic and Protestant leaders falsely accused women of witchcraft, denying them a fair trial and then torturing them, burning them or drowning them. Later Christians resisted efforts to grant women the right to own property, leaving them destitute if they were divorced or their husbands died. During the 1800s, church leaders opposed allowing women to pursue higher education. In the United States church leaders were opposed to give women the right to vote.

Conservative denominations in recent years have demonized feminism and blamed all of society's ills on the feminist movement. Some Christians actually believe that the breakdown of the family is the fault of women demanding equal rights in the workplace. (The definition for feminist is someone who believes that women should have equality with men in political, economic and social situations.) We are all Divine beings regardless of sex, race, color, religion, creed, etc. Shouldn't we all be equal with equal rights in all situations?

In Latin America Christian church leaders regularly beat their wives. Guatemala has the worlds highest per capita rate of murders of women in the world. Nigeria has no laws against domestic abuse. Muslim women are often brutalized. In India women are known to commit suicide because they can't find protection from their husbands beatings.

A growing number of women are turning away from organized religion because it has marginalized them and does not protect them.

The modern Divine Feminine women are here on earth at this time to speak up and break patriarchal traditions that coax women to be submissive and obedient and only tend to mundane matters of hearth and home. It is time for the divine women to step forward and shake lose from the trapping of religious culture and step into their full potential of the Divine Feminine women they truly are.

## Masculine Energy's Control Over Women

Worldwide women are still considered second class, below men in status. Our society is still patriarchal. Most young women's first experience in sex is rape, weather forced or coerced. One out of five women will be raped in their lifetime. Sexual violence is really about a power imbalance between women and men.

The definition of rape is any sexual encounter that's unwanted or non-consensual, and when a woman or girl is coerced into having sex that she doesn't want to have, that is still considered a rape.

More than 26% of rape victims said they were physically threatened during the encounter, 46% said they were physically held down. Over half (56%) of them said they were verbally pressured into having sex, and 16% said that their partner threatened to end the relationship if they didn't have sex.

Women who were forced to have sex the first time were also more likely to report having had an abortion and have had problems ovulating or menstruating, significantly higher than women who described their first sexual experience as consensual.

According to a CDC survey "Often, the sexual violence happens when the women were girls. 7% said they were younger than 10 at the time of the assault, while another 29% said they were between the ages of 11 and 14. The largest segment, at 39% were girls between 15 and 17 years old.

Women experience violence in many ways, from physical abuse to sexual assault and from financial abuse to sexual harassment or trafficking. Whatever form it takes, to include verbal and emotional abuse, violence against women can have serious long-term physical and emotional effects.

Girls and women who have been abused can be left with a very unhealthy view of sex. It is viewed as a loss of power and domination men have over them. Instead of pleasure it is associated with pain. They may learn to use their sexuality against men to punish and use them and never learn to love or trust them. They may be forever robbed of the divinity and sacredness that the union between a man and woman can be.

As women many of us resist our femininity because we grow up in a society which leads us to believe it is better to be born a boy. We are objectified and many of us are brutalized. We are taught that there is shame in the functions of our female bodies. We are made to believe that there are just certain unfortunate things that come along with being born a girl that we must accept because they are our "cross to bear".

The rites of passage when a girl begins her menses, experiences love and heartbreak, motherhood and menopause, too often happen in shame and secrecy.

This is the opposite of our ancient ancestors who honored women, the beauty of their bodies and their monthly cycles for what they stood for. Women's bodies were seen as sacred and women as Goddesses because she literally gave birth to life and nurtured it through childhood.

# Archaic Structures Breaking Down

There is no denying the political, medical, financial and media systems have an agenda of their own, which has nothing to do with taking care of the people. Environmental and political crises are forcing a reevaluation of our culture. We are faced with the necessity and opportunity of evolving a new social structure. If we are to survive social unrest, destruction of the rainforests, pollution of the land, water and environment, cruelty to animals and one another, extinction of animals and sea life, we are going to have to resurrect the values once associated with female-based religious systems;

- values of kindness
- compassion and healing
- of providing and sheltering
- of nourishing
- of holding all life sacred to include the earth, all living creatures and the plant kingdom
- and most of all love for humanity

The ancient people lived in accordance with Earth's natural rhythms and cycles. Everything was considered sacred: plants, animals, the earth itself, and women and men alike, and thus they lived in harmony with life.

Nearly all of the memorable encounters with The Divine recorded in myth and history occurred in a natural setting, the wilderness, the garden, a mountain top, the desert, but seldom in a cathedral.

We humans have become blind to our connection to Mother Earth as we rush to cut down the forests, mine the mountains, and frack everything else in between. We are destroying the habitats of wild creatures and plant medicine, and making much of the world uninhabitable. We don't realize or even seem to care that we are damaging the web of life, the planet that gives us life, ultimately, ourselves. The reason for this is our disconnection to nature. When we are disconnected from the natural world we lose our ability to feel empathy for her and see the big picture of what is going on. We have lost the connection to the feminine energy that binds us together and our hearts often become numb.

Our present social and religious structures are archaic and beginning to dissolve and break down.

Old religions are crumbling and women are breaking out of the shackles of outdated patriarchal systems. Women are becoming brave enough to speak their truth without fear of persecution or at least being put to death.

Every woman has a mysterious force within her, an ancient wisdom that is always whispering. She has a divine holy force that has been contained and restricted for millennia but is ready to rise again.

There is still much work to be done and that is why we, The Divine Feminine, are here on earth at this time, to use our intuitive, nourishing, loving, intelligent feminine nature and stand up together and bring corrective balance into our world.

The world needs women to wake up their Divine Feminine power and take their rightful place next to the Divine Masculine (there are many) to balance out the energies which have spun out of control.

Collectively, we will intentionally bring back Divine Feminine Energy into our troubled world. The return of the Divine Feminine Energy working side by side with the Divine Masculine Energy is essential to the maturation of human spirituality.

There is no more "Behind a great man is a great woman". If you were great you wouldn't be behind him! If he was great he wouldn't put himself in front of you. Truth be told, it puts too much pressure on a man to carry such a heavy burden. A good man would appreciate a good woman by his side, being with him, not behind him. A Divine Feminine is not next to the masculine to protect him or further his agenda, she is beside him to protect humanity and Mother Earth and balance the masculine energy with Divine Feminine Energy.

# CHAPTER 6

## The Unseen World

*"We are all visitors of this time, this place. We are just passing through. Our purpose is to observe, to learn, to grow, to love, and then we return home". Australian Aboriginal Proverb*

The unseen world is also called the spirit world, heaven, the other world, invisible world, and paradise. It is the belief we came from another place before we came to earth and there is a place we go when we leave this life.

## Mystics

A mystic is one who senses more to life than making a living or being of service in the world, although these things are both necessary and good.

Scott Peck (psychiatrist, author of The Road Less Traveled) says, 'Mystics, are people who have seen a kind of cohesion beneath the surface of things'. They recognize and embrace the mystery of life. From every culture and religion, Mystics have referred to unity, also, to community. They're comfortable with paradox, and often explore paradoxical ideas in their work.

Mystics understand that the more they discover about life, the more new mysteries they will uncover. They are comfortable with the idea, that we may never know the "Truth" of the universe.

Mystics acknowledge that the universe is infinite and mysterious and is far too complex for the human mind to fully comprehend. They don't know everything and they know they don't know everything. Mystics enjoy reaching out, learning new things and hearing new perspectives. They trust in the universe's plan and see their journey as one of understanding, not preaching.

An example of a mystic would be Baruch de Spinoza, a Dutch philosopher of the 17th century. When Albert Einstein was often asked if he believed in God he would always reply "I believe in the God of Spinoza." Spinoza wrote:

"God would say:

Stop praying. What I want you to do is go out into the world and enjoy your life. I want you to sing, have fun and enjoy everything I've made for you.

Stop going into those dark, cold temples that you built yourself and saying they are my house. My house is in the mountains, in the woods, rivers, lakes, beaches. That's where I live and there I express my love for you.

Stop blaming me for your miserable life; I never told you there was anything wrong with you or that you were a sinner, or that your sexuality was a bad thing. Sex is a gift I have given you and with which you can express your love, your ecstasy, your joy. So don't blame me for everything they made you believe.

Stop reading alleged sacred scriptures that have nothing to do with me. If you can't read me in a sunrise, in a landscape, in the look of your friends, in your son's eyes, you will find me in no book!

Stop asking me "will you tell me how to do my job?" Stop

being so scared of me. I do not judge you or criticize you, nor get angry, or bothered. I am pure love.

Stop asking for forgiveness, there's nothing to forgive. If I made you, I filled you with passions, limitations, pleasures, feelings, needs, inconsistencies, free will. How can I blame you if you respond to something I put in you? How can I punish you for being the way you are, if I'm the one who made you? Do you think I could create a place to burn all my children who behave badly for the rest of eternity? What kind of god would do that?

Respect your peers and don't do what you don't want for yourself. All I ask is that you pay attention in your life, that alertness is your guide.

My beloved, this life is not a test, not a step on the way, not a rehearsal, nor a prelude to paradise. This life is the only thing here and now and it is all you need.

I have set you absolutely free, no prizes or punishments, no sins or virtues, no one carries a marker, no one keeps a record.

You are absolutely free to create in your life. Heaven or hell.

I can't tell you if there's anything after this life but I can give you a tip. Live as if there is not. As if this is your only chance to enjoy, to love, to exist.

So, if there's nothing after, then you will have enjoyed the opportunity I gave you. And if there is, rest assured that I won't ask if you behaved right or wrong, I'll ask. Did you like it? Did you have fun? What did you enjoy the most? What did you learn?

Stop believing in me; believing is assuming, guessing, imagining. I don't want you to believe in me. I want you to believe in you. I want you to feel me in you when you kiss your beloved, when you tuck in your little girl, when you caress your dog, when you bathe in the sea.

Stop praising me. What kind of egomaniac God do you think I am? I'm bored being praised. I'm tired of being thanked. Feeling grateful? Prove it by taking care of yourself, your health, your relationships, the world. Express your joy! That's the way to praise me.

Stop complicating things and repeating as a parakeet what you've been taught about me.

What do you need more miracles for? So many explanations?

The only thing for sure is that you are here, that you are alive, that this world is full of wonders."

## Animism

Animism is the belief that all things have a spirit or soul, including the earth, animals, plants, rivers, mountains, stars, the moon, and the sun. Animism has been practiced since ancient times. Animism is a belief or practice, not a religion. Though many ancient religions, indigenous people and shamans practice it as a part of their religion. They see earth as a living being rather than how to make money from her.

## Magic

The ancients did not have the benefit of science to have an understanding of how many things worked. If they didn't understand how or why something happened they thought it was magic and therefore they were very superstitious.

In Medieval times the city dwelling populace no longer understood herbalism and natural healing methods. It was easy for the church to convince them these things were evil witchcraft in order to justify killing off the country dweller who would not convert. But what is it that was considered witchcraft?

- Herbalism, plant medicine
- Being a strong independent woman
- Female healers who used natural remedies

- Midwives
- Women who were attractive
- Women who were old and feeble, and anyone who stood up for them or befriended them
- The practice of non-Christian rituals and practices
- The beliefs of other cultures

Today we have more knowledge of the world and the universe but it is still very limited. When something fantastical happens that we don't understand, we don't call it magic anymore, we call it a miracle.

## Myths

"Myths are universal and timeless stories that reflect and shape our lives. They explore our desires, our fears, our longings, and provide narratives that remind us what it mean to be human". Karen Armstrong

Myths are stories that were passed down through the ages as a teaching tool, which may or may not have been true. The ancients were great story tellers and teachers which kept their history and traditions alive.

Pre-history is the time before written language to record history. Knowledge was handed down from one generation to the next verbally with no written record to prove or disprove the story.

## Religion

It is not my intention to try to invalidate your beliefs, values, religion or lifestyle. I am not trying to convince you of anything I personally may or may not believe in. My intention is to give you permission to question your beliefs and opinions that don't bring you joy or feel right to you any more. Religion can be a tricky subject because many of us grew up being told not to question our religion.

In most religious cultures we are taught to not question our church elders or parents and not to socially associate with people outside of our faith. Many times we are not allowed to go to church with or date school friends who are not of the same faith we are. We can even be a little afraid and suspicious of people outside our religious communities.

As a result we grow up with a narrow view of the world. As adults we can end up being very naive or ignorantly closed minded and opinionated, with very little first hand knowledge or experience of the outside world.

On the other hand we may rebel from being so controlled and micro managed that once we get our freedom we go wild to the opposite extreme.

At some point many of us find we are not happy with our life circumstances that we created out of our young belief system. If we stay in our situation, not believing we have a choice or the capability to change, we can become depressed or angry or feel victimized and blame everyone else for our misery, making everyone around us miserable and our situation worse.

The state in which I currently reside sells more anti-depressants and ice cream than any other. The states culture is centered around a religion which is very patriarchal. This is a problem for women who are restless, and want more independence and control over their own life. According to this states Domestic Violence Coalition, domestic violence, sexual assault and stalking by an intimate partner, which are reported, are one in three adult women over the age of 18.

Women here tend to have a lot of children, not much education, low wages and many times no where to turn for help which is a dangerous cocktail for high domestic violence homicide rates. The impact on women is real; it makes them feel degraded, fearful, worthless and dispensable.

This state and the predominate religion here is not unique, I only use it as an example because it is the one I am most familiar with. The Christian patriarchal thinking that women should be obedient and subservient to their husbands in all situations, has been ingrained in our minds by all religions. This kind of gender prejudice also teaches that women can't be fulfilled or spiritually effective without a husband and children. And that God created women as inferior beings, designed to serve their husbands.

This is nothing more than religious chauvinism, it is wrong and it is all lies. The male led churches have lied to women about their worth and value in God's eyes. Faulty biblical interpretation has caused much suffering to women, manipulating them into a place of powerlessness.

This low view of women is rooted in the misconception in the bible, that the first woman, Eve, was created by God as an inferior creature with less strength, mental capacity and spiritual giftedness and was meant to be in a state of subordination to Adam. And then there is the idea that Eve was deceived by the serpent so she and her daughters must forever be punished.

The fact that she was presented to Adam to help him does not make her inferior. God said it is not good for man to be alone, acknowledging that Adam was in an inferior condition, a state of incompleteness without a mate to stand at his side as his equal. They enjoyed equal access to God and Eve could communicate with the Lord in the same way as Adam.

It is no wonder that so many Christian women suffer with low self esteem, depression and eating disorders. It is no wonder that religious homes in the United States are ranked among the highest for domestic abuse, second only to the homes of alcoholics.

Divine Feminine Energy is nurturing and protective which makes women good mothers. But it is a cultural bias, not a spiritual or scientific principle that women are made for the kitchen and laundry room. Many women enjoy fulfilling the role of a stay at home mother, there is no greater calling, but it is not every woman's inclination nor should it be her only acceptable option.

This is an area in which Divine Feminine Energy will bring spiritual liberation to women. Not by overthrowing men and putting women in a place of superiority but by throwing off the shackles of religious chauvinism and patriarchy and help men and women work together side by side, at home, at work and at church, if they wish.

You may have bought into the view that there are limits on what you can do. People of smaller vision may want you to stay in your place. Unfortunately, many women have embraced the idea of being a Christian doormat and subservience is part of their identity that has become a place of security for them. Ultimately what you believe rules you. If you believe your purpose is to fill limited roles, you will fill them and stop there, never knowing what more was available for you.

You were created with a unique destiny that only you will be able to fulfill. Many of you reading this are spiritual but not affiliated with any particular religion per say, but if you are religious and affiliated with a church, you can be a huge service to your Divine Feminine sisters in your religion by speaking up and questioning injustices to women being taught or practiced in your church. You do not have to leave your church to help right the wrongs going on around you.

## Religion vs Spirituality

In our world, there are many religions and they all preach that their story is the right story. Religion's dogma is a set of rules that must be followed for your salvation. It tells you who is good and who is bad. Dotted throughout religion there is a lot of fear. Fear of the consequences of your actions, fear of what might happen after you die, if you don't live your life accordingly. I do believe that all religions have golden threads of truth woven in them and that many people can be both truly beautiful souls and religious at the same time, but ultimately anything that separates us, creates fear or division is not good for our souls and is definitely not good for the greater good of humankind.

Spirituality is perhaps the most natural thing there is: it is simply your own conscious-self recognizing that you are more than just a body, that you are a soul with infinite potential. As opposed to following a specific ideology or a set of rules, spirituality simply lets you follow your heart, it encourages you to listen to your intuition and do what is right for yourself and others around you. It truly sets you free to be the best you can be and to be a good person with no promise of punishment or reward. The reward is simply your own inner happiness.

## Organized Religion

Organized religions around the world are no longer heart centered, they are dogmatic, convinced they are right and disapproving of those who don't agree. Today more and more women are questioning the old outdated belief systems in their cultures and religions. Many women are leaving organized religions that they no longer relate to. But some are staying associated with their religion because they feel more comfortable staying with their family and community, however they are awake and disregard the teachings they do not find truth in.

I am not suggesting that if you identify with being spiritual you can't also be religious or that in order to be awakened you should leave organized religion, or if you are a feminist you must worship a Goddess religion rather than a male God religion.

Organized religion is not the belief you should be worried about. No matter your religion, faith or belief you should take the time to look within yourself and discover what you believe, what you love and what offends you. Don't be afraid to question everything. Don't be afraid to read books and go to different churches and organizations you may have never considered before. When we first awaken to our spiritual self and learn about the history of the early church and patriarchal religions it is easy to abandon organized religion all together, but that may leave you feeling lost and lonely. Where do you go when you no longer believe in or trust organized religion?

Too many people step away from faith simply because their new found tribe tells them it isn't vouge to be religious in this day and time. You need to find the church, organization, religion or spiritual family that is right for you. By questioning and exploring what is in your heart and the many options you have, some people find a new "home" and others return to their original spiritual home with renewed faith and devotion.

Humans are tribal by nature and we long to belong and be a part of a community, cause or family. We long to be loved, appreciated and helpful to others. Being around like-minded people helps us to learn, grow, communicate, understand different perspectives and be better humans.

## Remember Your Divinity

> *"Woman, you are far more than just someone who walks on the earth, you are a soul. A divine being. An all-powerful creator. Within you dwells the infinite wisdom of the ages and the holy creative force of the wild feminine. You are sacred, accept nothing else but the divine". Shikoba*

As divine women we need to re-wild ourselves and remember our divinity. Male dominance has tried to tame us and the patriarchal society has tried to control us. We were not meant to be property, abused or dominated.

As soon as we awaken to these truths we have to ingrain in our daughters their divine value and their rights in this world. We have to teach our sons to respect, support and protect women, not dominate, use and control them.

We have to stand up for ourselves and be good examples to the new generations to come and not allow ourselves to be treated poorly or disrespected. We teach by example not words.

## Awakening Your Spiritual Self

*Imagine a woman who embodies spirituality. A woman who honors her body as the Sacred Temple of the Spirit of Life. Who breathes deeply as a prayer of gratitude for life itself. You are that woman.*

The Divine Feminine exists in the world of the spirit. It can best be accessed by seeking it through thoughtful prayer and sincere meditation. You don't have to deliver any lofty prayers. You don't have to become a Zen master. Just talk to the God of your understanding and let God talk to you.

God is also called the Higher Power, Spirit, the Creator, the Universe, Source and vaguely as the powers that be.

Do meditations aimed specifically at connecting to your sacred femininity. There is no wrong way to do this. One of the best ways to pray and meditate is to go outside and connect to Mother Earth (or Mother Nature), which is probably the most internationally recognized symbol of the Divine Feminine. Sit on the grass, enjoy the flowers, lean against a tree, feel the sunshine, listen to the birds singing. It might seem weird if you are not a nature lover. But, once you begin to really soak up the power of the outdoors, you will start to feel it in your soul.

## Limiting Beliefs

As women our cultural and religious teachings have NOT taught us that we are powerful, sacred, and glorious. We are trained by society to think we aren't smart enough, pretty enough, thin enough, worthy enough, strong enough, courageous enough, etc. We put limits on ourselves because we have bought into this false belief system of who we are and who we are not.

Just remember our first mothers and grandmothers on earth, of whom we are descendants, were the spiritual leaders, healers and teachers that journeyed into the spirit world. They did it and so can we, it's in our DNA! They were powerful and so are we. Nothing has changed that.

## Your Higher Self

Our physical body is just the tip of the iceberg when it comes to what makes us, "us". We all have a soul, which is also called your Higher Self. Your Higher Self is the purest form of you. It is everything love and never concerns itself with trivial things. She's been around for a LONG time, and knows the ways of the Universe. She also knows why you're here! We can connect to our Higher Self through our intuition and meditation. Close your eyes and look within.

Your higher self is also called your soul, your spirit, your inner goddess, the essence of who you are.

Your Higher Self understands that there is only life after life, that death is a brief change in status from the visible to an invisible existence. You are both a physical being and a spiritual being. It is possible to experience the cosmos first hand, across the furthest reaches of space and beyond time, without dying, and returning to your physical existence. You can be the architect of your own destiny with the information you bring back with you.

The only thing that will stop you from communicating with the unseen world, your spirit guides and guardian angels and receiving personal revelation is the belief that you can't or shouldn't.

## The Veil Between Two Worlds

The subconscious is recognized as the source of creativity, intuition, inspiration, inner knowing, interconnectedness, and spiritual enlightenment. Within this realm reality shifts and expands, creating a matrix that is far more elastic and multi-dimensional than is perceived by the conscious mind. When we access and spend time within the subconscious we are released from the confines of our logical, practical mind. The messages we receive from our dreams and the primordial symbols, or archetypes handed down to us from our ancestors, inform us about what is unique, authentic, and sacred to each of us. When we heed these messages we are following the path of our soul's evolution. Beyond our conscious mind and usual senses the veil is lifted, revealing a world of unlimited possibilities.

Indeed, we can walk in both the physical world and the spirit realms. We can maintain a viable relationship with our guides, friends, and loved ones who dwell in Spirit. We can relate to them just as we do with friends and family here in the physical world. It is not only possible, it is normal and natural to do so because we ourselves are spiritual beings, even if we are temporarily encased in physical bodies.

- If you could visit the spirit world yourself, without the need of a medium, priest, shaman or prophet, would you want to learn how?
- If you could part the veil between earth and the spirit world who would you want to see?

- What questions would you ask?
- What would you want to know?
- How would it change your life?

The good news is that you can learn how and some humans have had the gift and ability to do so from the beginning of time. The old sages understood that there never was a locked gate between us and the invisible world. The invisible world exists alongside the visible one, ever present and accessible. We can bring its wisdom into our world at any time to provide healing and balance.

- We can contact loved ones who have already transitioned back to "the other side." We find we are not really separated from them after all. They are happy. Our grieving can end.
- We can learn there is no real reason to fear anything here in the physical world, including misfortune, accidents, illness, or even death of our physical bodies.
- We can re-discover that life on "the other side" is just as real, if not more real, than life here in the physical world.
- We can discover that we are, in fact, spiritual beings and that our real home lies in the spirit realms.
- We can re-discover the lessons we pre-planned for our current life while still in Spirit before coming to earth.

Throughout history there have been mediums, psychics, seers, shamans, prophets, holy and lay people who have had the gift of being able to communicate with angels and spirits on the other side and some can see the auras of humans. Our aura is an electromagnetic field of energy that extends all around our body for about 4-5 feet. It radiates the health of our physical, mental, emotional, as well as spiritual energies, often including various colors.

These gifted people have often remained in the shadows, on the outskirts of society to avoid clashes with Christian religions.

The original Christian Fathers took away and forbade it's followers any practices that gave them independent thought in order to control them. It's followers were dependent on the church to provide all guidance, blessings and forgiveness. They smeared and demonized those who would claim to have the ability to reach the heavens and communicate with God, angels and spirits.

## You Are Not Alone, You Have More Help than You Know

*"Walking I am listening to a deeper way. Suddenly all my Ancestors are behind me. Be still they say. Watch and Listen. You are the result of the Love of Thousands." - Linda Hogan*

The truth is, from the beginning, we were never placed on earth alone without help from the spirit world, our spirit guides and guardian angels, and the knowledge of how to get in touch with them.

In the beginning we lived in small communities protected and guided by the shamans who visited the spirit world for us and brought back knowledge for our happiness and health, our purpose for being here, and reassurance that we are not alone, which they taught and told in stories that we could understand and relate to at the time.

When necessary about 50% of the tribe could journey into the unseen world to get assistance when they were without their shaman. Everyone's genealogy eventually takes them back to the original indigenous people, meaning we have the gift and ability to journey to the unseen world, because it is in our DNA, and because that has always been the plan.

We can get direct revelation for ourselves. We can part the veil between the visible and invisible world. We don't have to be perfect and we don't have to be worthy, chosen or ordained or have special gifts or powers.

Placing a veil across our memory of who we are is a part of the plan of our earthly journey and our purpose for being here. I use to think this was so unfair when I believed life was a test and our existence in the next life was solely based on how well we did here on earth. You cannot believe God is a very loving God when you live in fear of his judgements and punishments. Religion has always ruled with fear to keep people in line.

I have come to understand that we are here to have an earthly experience not an extended spiritual experience. We need to have a balance between actually living our human life and praying, meditating and journeying to the spirit world, though it is doable and helpful, spending too much time there takes away from our earthly purpose. We come from the spirit world and we will return there when our earthy life is over. Now is the time to have a physical body and experience a human life for our edification and growth toward becoming Gods and Goddesses like our heavenly parents.

## Spirit Guides and Angels

We all have Spirit Guides and helpers and they're wonderful. Spirit Guides are the spirits that help guide us throughout our journey in life. They communicate with you through your intuition, whispers and prompts to provide you with Divine guidance. You might have Guides that help you with parenting, gardening, academic pursuits, your psychic journey, and anything else you need!

We all have a spirit team that will divinely guide us, without ever imposing on our free will. Your team is made up firstly of your inner goddess, and angels, spirit guides, ancestors, loved ones, teachers, and ascended masters. Their sole job is to guide you toward your most authentic and fulfilled life. They will communicate with you using your natural psychic abilities, intuition, prayer, dreams, epiphanies and meditation.

## Meditation

Meditation is as old as humanity itself, the Neanderthals, Shamans, Taoist China and Buddhist India, The Torah (the first five books of the Tanakh, the Hebrew Bible) contains a description of the patriarch Isaac going to 'lasuach' in a field. This term is generally understood as being some form of meditation. Buddhist monks and Christian Monks practice meditation for years to get to the trance-like state where they can receive enlightenment. Shamans use a trance-like meditation to enter the unseen world.

## Meditation is Backed by Science

Meditation is a precise technique for resting the mind and attaining a state of consciousness that is totally different from the normal waking state. It is the means for experiencing the center of consciousness within. Meditation is not a part of any religion; it is a science, which means that the process of meditation follows a particular order, has definite principles, and produces results that can be verified.

The practice, by itself, can be an invaluable tool in healing, stress reduction, personal revelation and meeting your spiritual helpers. Whether you adhere to a particular faith or not is irrelevant, millions of people all over the world believe that meditation is the way to clear your mind of extraneous thoughts so you can listen to your soul, your spirit guides and God.

There are many forms of meditation. There is no one way, right way or wrong way to meditate. Whichever way works for you is the right way.

When you meditate and your right brain and left brain are slowly vibrating in unison (entrained) in the theta state, clear and relaxed, is when you can receive enlightenment or journey into the unseen worlds. Your spirit helpers will be waiting for you and happy to help you.

What you see, hear, feel or intuit will depend on how you learn and relate. Some of us are visual learners, others are auditory and learn better when we hear things, others are telepathic, and others are more intuitive and have an instant knowing. Your guides, teachers, helpers and angels will relate to you and appear to you in a way that you personally can understand and relate to.

Anyone can meditate and everyone can access the spirit world. The heavens are open to all, we don't have to earn it or deserve it. We are loved, we are welcome, we are worthy and not judged.

## Ancient Spiritual Practices Included Meditation

**Shamanism:** One of the core principles of Shamanism is meditation, which they call journeying. Shamanism is not a religion it is a spiritual way of living life. The shamans practice of direct revelation is the ancestral precursor of all our religious and philosophical traditions, both ancient and modern.

Shamanism was the first spiritual belief system on earth and has remained in tact with the few indigenous cultures remaining on the earth today. Until recently they have been very secretive and protective of their rites and ceremonies. But their prophecy tells them they will not be on the earth for much longer and they need to teach the outsiders the shamanistic ways for future survival. They believe the earth is in such a turmoil that we as individuals, not just the shamans, need to learn the shamanistic ways to help ourselves, our families and communities. They see not only humans are in danger but animals and Mother Earth, as well.

**Buddhism:** Buddhism is not a religion it is a philosophy and a way of living your life. The main principle of Buddhism is meditation.

Buddha spent 6 years in deep meditation trying to find the answers to end his own suffering and he brought back to humanity the means to end their suffering in the face of disease, old age, and death. After his enlightenment he spent the next 45 years teaching what he had learned.

**Hinduism:** Hinduism is the world's third largest religion after Christianity and Islam. Hindus often focus on individual disciplines such as meditation, yoga, chants, and the burning of incense to deities.

Hinduism emerged in South Asia around 2000 BCE, thousands of years before Jesus or Muhammad lived. And unlike the religious movements those men started, Hinduism claims no single founder or triggering event.

## How Do We Do It?

As our main topic is women's ancient spiritual heritage we will focus on the ancient shamanic meditation of journeying. There is not a right way or a wrong way, it is a skill that improves with practice. It will deepen and grow as you continue to practice and establish a long term relationship with your helping spirits.

Before you begin your meditation you will want to turn off your phone and find a place you will not be disturbed. It is good to put something over your eyes to block out the light or close the blinds, shades or curtains. The shaman is called "one who sees in the dark". Some people light a candle in the room or burn incense to create a sacred space. Some people like total quiet, others like soft music and others prefer the monotonous beat of shamanic drumming. The shamanistic ritual of beating the drum is the thread guiding the shaman to the invisible world and back to the natural world.

Set an intention in advance as this will set up a drawing power for that which you are seeking. For example you might ask for guidance in your life, in a relationship, your health, an answer to a prayer, or your work. Or you could ask a question that will help you grow and evolve, such as "What should I focus my life on right now?" or "What are my gifts?" or "What is my purpose on earth at this time?" Or you could ask to meet your guardian angel or spirit guides, or an ancestor.

Another way to entreat the help of your spirit guides is by asking them to perform a healing to alleviate the pain of a physical or emotional issue you are dealing with. Many people report profound healing when they ask a helping spirit to perform a healing on them. It is definitely worth trying.

While meditating bring to mind any situation that is currently concerning you. Call on your higher self to guide you. Ask your intuitive knowing to rise up within you and reveal the most resonant path for your soul to flourish. Spend as long here as you need, allowing ample time for the answers to come. When you are finished, lie down to relax, receive and assimilate the effects of your practice.

Search to see if there is a shaman in your community who can teach you how to journey or if there are any groups that journey together on a regular basis. YouTube has some good shaman drumming recordings you can use if you are going solo. There are books that teach how to Journey and some have CDs of shamanic drumming included. See Resources in the back of the book.

Meditating and meditative journeying are wonderful ways of accessing spiritual wisdom. It is said that prayer is asking and in the stillness of meditating is receiving the answers.

# Navigating the Physical World with Your Intuition

*"We live on a blue planet that circles around
a ball of fire next to a moon that moves the
sea, and you don't believe in miracles?"*

You are a soul, a spiritual being having an earthly experience. To accomplish that, your soul must inhabit a physical body. This is a new experience for us and I am sure harder than we thought it was going to be when we agreed and prepared to come here to earth.

Our spirit, our soul, our higher self has lived a long time and is intelligent, experienced, powerful and sacred. Our intuition at times is our higher self communicating with us and sometimes it is our guardian angel or spirit guides. Some of us have a thinner veil across our mind and are naturally more intuitive than others. But we all have the capability to be intuitive.

When you get a feeling that you should do something, and you don't follow through, and it turns out that is exactly what you should have done, and you could kick yourself for not listening to yourself. That is intuition. The more you listen to yourself and follow through without questioning, the stronger your intuition will be and you will experience it more often.

In the beginning of developing your intuition you think that your inner knowing, feelings, or thoughts, may just be a passing thought and not have any validity, keeping you from acting on it. Or fear that you have no explanation other than a gut feeling for your thoughts may keep you from following through. But if you keep practicing and keep listening to yourself you will learn to not question your prompts and you will be confident enough to not feel like you have to explain yourself to anyone.

Here is where words are unnecessary to communicate or convey a message. The symbol, the representational picture or image, conveys the complete thought, concept, or ideal without the use of words to describe it; the proverbial, "a picture is worth a thousand words." This idea is tremendously powerful, just as the way we "talk" to ourselves, our inner language, the way we know who we are, does not come from words, but rather from the timeless source within that knows who we are.

Intuition is one of the gifts we were given to compensate for that veil placed over our memory of who we really are and where we came from. The ability to meditate and go deep within ourselves to find answers is another gift. Journeying to the spirit world for guidance and healing is another of the gifts we have to help us navigate through this human physical world.

## Ancient Spiritual Beliefs

*"The old religion is the magic of the earth itself.*
*It is the essence which binds all things together.*
*It will last long beyond the time of men."*

- Our ancient ancestors did not have religion, they had spirituality.
- They believed in a spiritual mother and father.
- They believed every living thing has a spirit, to include Mother Earth.
- They believed in life after death.
- They believed in angels, the spirit world and spirit guides.
- They believed in personal revelation.
- They believed in gratitude.
- They believed in community.
- They believed in rituals and ceremonies.

- They believed we each find our own way and were not burdened or forced to follow others beliefs or opinions of a particular persuasion.
- They shared, they talked, they discussed but ultimately they were free to find their own path to happiness and back to Spirit.

# CHAPTER 7

## Reconnect With Mother Earth

*"Live in each season as it passes; breathe the air, drink the drink, taste the fruit, and resign yourself to the influence of the earth." Henry David Thoreau*

In ancient times, we humans were keenly attuned to the heartbeat of the planet. Life was lived on the edge. Our survival as a species depended on our ability to live in harmony with the earth.

Our ancient ancestors believed the earth has a living spirit. They called her mother earth because she nourished them and gave them everything they needed to live. They loved her and thanked her every day. They thanked the sun for giving them warmth. They thanked the water for satisfying their thirst and healing them. They thanked the plants and animals for feeding them. They were children of the earth.

Our inner divinity recognizes that we are profoundly intertwined with nature, its mysteries and miracles. Too many of us today unconsciously tune out our deep connection to nature and our natural state of inner knowing and don't listen to the whisperings of the earth, our intuition or our Creator. When we do listen we have a greater sense of emotional well-bing and relax into our natural state of "knowing".

Mother Nature is the ultimate divine energy, by spending more time with her you will instantly connect with your Inner Goddess. Just sitting outside will reduce your blood pressure and help you feel immediately peaceful and calm. Release all your thoughts and worries into nature and you will see how she will care for you and heal you.

Answer your call to the wild and get outside and reconnect with Mother Nature, any way you can, anytime you can. Don't wait until you have the time or energy. Just do it regularly! We have much research that shows the tremendous effect nature has on your mental and physical health. Human beings were meant to be nourished and fed by nature. Your mind, body, and soul need it. Reconnect with Mother Nature every time you are outside. The wind blowing is energizing you, the sun is energizing you, and trees are sending you oxygen, beauty, and shade. The birds, butterflies, flowers and other natural elements are tantalizing all your senses.

Never in history have we been so far from merging with the natural world and so separated from nature. According to a study sponsored by the Environmental Protection Agency, the average American spends 93% of his or her time indoors. But the good news is that even a small amount of time in nature can have an impact on our health. Being in nature can restore our mood, give us back our energy and vitality, refresh and rejuvenate us.

Recent discoveries in neuroscience have proven that more than 50% of the heart is comprised of neural cells. It is from our hearts that we process our energetic connection to everything we come in contact with. The problem is that we have cut ourselves off from this connection to nature by allowing ourselves to be distracted by technology and all of its associated noise. We cannot hear it if we are not listening.

We need to spend more time unplugged and find ways to let nature balance our lives. Find small openings for nature every day, whether in the country or the city, at home, in the workplace, in schools and in neighborhoods;

- Plant native species in your backyard and leave part of it wild
- take kids fishing and hiking
- build a bird feeder or go bird watching
- walk in the park
- ride a bike
- set up a community garden
- have a picnic
- exercise outdoors

A great idea is to walk barefoot in the grass and close your eyes to ultimately feel connected with the earth beneath your feet. This activity is called Earthing and it's my personal favorite. Having physical contact with the surface of the Earth will make you feel fully renewed and it will restore your balance fast.

Connecting with Mother Nature on a daily basis will help you become a strong healthy woman and the true Goddess you are!

## Connect with Plants

The consciousness of plants may be vastly different from our understanding of consciousness. Interacting with plants is not simply about talking to them. It is much more about opening the lines of communication with them on an energetic level and sharing our life-force. By opening our hearts and experiencing nature in its fullness we can begin to realize this connection. It is a purely experiential experience. We have to spend time in nature to truly feel it.

Understanding our connection with the earth through the wisdom of plants helps each of us to find and maintain our own unique, delicate balance. Plants affect us in remarkable ways, physically, emotionally, spiritually, and psychically. By understanding the transformation that plants can effect in us, then working with them in whatever ways are most appropriate, we begin to tap into their deeply-rooted wisdom.

A personal, practical knowledge of plants and their uses has always been part of the life skills for traditional people. Exploring nature's green realm and deepening our intimate connections with the power of plants is what our ancient ancestor did.

We need to bring back the ancient wisdom of medicine and food from the earth. Pick your food and medicine from your backyard. Make your own teas, brews, tinctures, brews and salves. Turn your kitchen into your alchemy laboratory. Bring back the wisdom that our divine ancestors carried.

## Grounding / Earthing

*"Forget not that the earth delights to feel*
*your bare feet and the winds long to play*
*with your hair."* Kahlil Gibran

Spirit and souls don't have physical bodies weighing them down, so their energetic vibe is super fast! Because of that, connecting with your intuitive abilities can leave you feeling like you're floating or drifting. Grounding simply reconnects you to the earth, and your spiritual self to your physical self.

How often do you see the sky, touch the earth, and gaze at distant mountains? You are part of the ever-growing, changing, and expanding world of Nature, even though modern technology tries to suggest otherwise. Stress comes from being ungrounded when you lose your connection to Mother Earth. Happiness and peace come from immersing yourself in the sights, sounds, scents, and textures of the outdoors.

Grounding or Earthing is defined as placing one's bare feet on the ground whether it be dirt, grass, sand or concrete, especially when humid or wet.

The basic principle of earthing is that you will be able to receive energy from the ground when you're in direct contact with a natural surface. In modern city life we no longer have direct physical contact with the Earth, and therefore are losing out on health benefits of exchanging electrons with the surface of our planet.

Years of extensive research has shown that connecting to the Earth's natural energy, by walking barefoot on grass, sand, dirt or rock can diminish chronic pain, fatigue and other ailments that plague so many people today.

From a scientific perspective, the idea is that the earth has a mild negative charge to it. Over time, especially in modern life, our bodies build up a positive charge. Direct contact with the earth can even out this positive charge and return the body to a neutral state.

Throughout history humans have walked, sat and slept on the ground, cultivated their land with bare hands and spent a lot of their time being naturally grounded.

Many people don't have this contact with the earth anymore, and some experts wonder if this is a contributor to the many rising health problems we face today. As a population, we wear rubber shoes and live indoors. In theory, many of us could go years without directly touching the earth at all, even if we're outside.

To add to this, we are also bathed in a sea of un-natural man-made electronic radiation from household appliances, mobile phones, wi-fi, "smart" technologies, microwaves and cell towers, which bombard us continuously with excess free radical damage to our tissues and cells. The Earth's energy helps to knock these excess free radicals down so that your body can heal and repair naturally, as it is meant to. Therefore, to remain in Divine Feminine good health, it is imperative that we reconnect with this natural energy daily to counteract the damaging effects of our modern lifestyle.

Our bodies are like rechargeable batteries using the Earth and the Universe to recharge. The Earth helps us to heal and gives us everything we need to survive, and works with the Universe to connect to a spiritual energy that keeps our bodies moving on a daily basis. We have a constant flow of energy from our feet to our minds.

**Take Your Shoes Off:** Go barefoot outside for at least half-hour and see what a difference it makes on your pain or stress level. Sit, stand, lay or walk on grass, sand, dirt, or plain concrete. These are all conductive surfaces from which your body can draw the Earth's energy. Wood, carpet, asphalt, sealed or painted concrete and vinyl won't work and will block the flow of electrons as they are not conductive surfaces. Experience for yourself the healing energy of the Earth.

## Walking Meditation

This type of meditation has been practiced by many cultures, religions and spiritual traditions for thousands of years. Buddhist and Eastern spiritual traditions used walking meditation in combination with long periods of sitting meditation.

As with all meditation, the principal benefit is to bring one's awareness back to the present moment, rather than being absorbed in the events of the past or speculating about the future. This full awareness of the present moment, free from the distractions of the ego, is said to be the key to a truly peaceful state of mind. The more you practice mindfulness, the more you will be able to be mindfully present in your everyday life.

While a beautiful, peaceful, natural environment is the ideal place to practice walking meditation, it is quite possible to use it to achieve inner calm in noisy environments, such as an airport. It is often in such stressful settings that people have the greatest need for the peace that walking meditation may bring.

Walking meditation is a mindfulness practice that you do while walking. It is usually done at a slower pace than your regular walking for exercise. Unlike most meditation practices, it is done on the move with your eyes open, your body moving, and an awareness of your surrounding environment.

## Begin Your Waking Meditation

1.  Start by picking a route, somewhere out in nature works best but if you have to do city walking that is fine too. As you get more comfortable with the practice, you can also just walk freely and where your heart wants to take you, but to start, having a route can help.

2.  As you place your first foot on the ground, say a quiet "thank you" to yourself, and begin walking. As you walk, try to just observe the sights, smells, and sensations around you. Really look, really smell, really feel what is in front of you.

3.  If you notice any thoughts creeping in, switch your focus to the things that stand out to you, such as street signs, flowers, birds and so on. If you see something that catches your eye, allow yourself to look at it. Don't pass judgment or get lost in your thoughts about it, just observe.

4.  As you walk like this, you will start to become more mindful of your body and your breathing. If you feel any tension in your body just be gentle with yourself and try to soften into it using your breath. Try to breathe deeply and take nice long exhales.

5. When you reach your destination and as you take your final step, say a closing "thank you" quietly to yourself again.

Remember the idea is to make this effortless, so while you can take all these steps into consideration, the real art with this is just allowing yourself to be free in the moment.

Walking meditation is one of the most versatile forms of meditation, it can be performed just about anywhere at any pace. It's especially good for beginners because a physical action is easier to focus the mind on rather than sitting in complete silence.

If you would like to explore the practice of walking meditation further you should read the excellent pocket-sized books by Vietnamese Zen Master Thich Nhat Hanh The Long Road Turns to Joy: A Guide to Walking Meditation. Also, Walking Meditation: Peace is Every Step by Thich Nhat Hanh. These are great primers for getting started in this practice.

## Mobile Meditation

When you run along a path in the middle of the woods or laps in the gym for the eightieth repetition, focusing on completing the exercise pushes everything else out of your mind. Jogging and training can be called mobile meditation.

## Go to the Water

Water is a feminine element. Water is a cleansing, healing, psychic, and loving element. It is the feeling of friendship and love that pours over us when we are with our family, friends and loved ones as we participate in water activities. When we swim it is water that supports us, when we are thirsty, it is water that quenches our thirst and gives us life.

In it's psychic ability water can be used as a means of crying or as an object for meditation. Ancient women knew how to create miracle concoctions and powerful potions, including seductive elixirs and strong soaps to wash clothes in rivers. The eternal bond linking water and women is illustrated in paintings of women bent on river banks or canals, busy washing the world's dirt away.

Water unceasingly changes shapes and transforms itself. Beings and things are born of water. It is thus a model out of which everything can be born. Water, consequently, becomes a symbol of fertility that can be found in all the myths and all the religions.

Water is a living and spiritual matter, working as a mediator between humans and gods. Water often represents the border between this world and the other.

Water also possesses medicinal virtues. Some waters are recognized miraculous powers capable of healing the bodies. Water was the first magic on earth, before plants, rocks and stones, the first source of medicine was water. Drinking plenty of "living" water is one of the best healers for the body. The American Indians had a saying about any ailment, "take it to the water". Water is healing, transforming and sensitive. Water carries away pollution and purifies both in a physical and symbolical sense.

With the exception of a few places on earth such as hot springs and the warm pacific ocean, water in nature is cold. Our ancestors played, swam and bathed in cold water. Scientific evidence now shows, what the ancients knew, that cold water is healing and therapeutic.

Having a cold bath or showers helps to stimulate the blood flow. When you submerge yourself in cold water, the blood rushes through your vital organs, which in turn helps your heart muscle become more efficient.

Cold showers can help with high-intensity exercise, relax muscles, and prevent them from swelling and inflammation.

Cold water therapy stimulates the lymph vessels forcing the lymphatic system to rapidly pump lymph fluid in your entire body, getting rid of all the waste. It then triggers the immune system's white blood cells to fight against all the unwanted toxins in the fluid. In other words, cold water positively affects both the lymphatic and immune systems which boost your mood, energy, and health.

If you're experiencing irritated skin or itchiness because of hives, dermatitis, eczema, or another reason, a cold shower helps calm the skin and prevents further skin inflammation. Your nerves can't transmit two signals at once, for example when your skin is irritated and you're having a cold shower, the cold automatically overrides the itchiness and the discomfort of the skin.

Having a cold shower or bath every day has many health benefits when it comes to improving the quality of your skin and hair. Cold showers help tighten pores, soften skin and due to the blood circulation, it improves the texture of the skin. Since cold doesn't release oil as it does when having a warm shower, it also prevents scalp breakouts, greasiness, and hair dandruff. In return, this helps stimulate hair follicles and thick hair.

A 2017 study showed that ice-cold immersion can help treat depression and other mental disorders. If using cold immersion on a daily basis, along with other lifestyle changes, cold therapy can also be just as effective or perhaps more effective than a medical prescription for mental well-being.

Cold therapy will boost your blood flow and trigger your neurotransmitter keeping your body and mind happy. Whether you are swimming, taking a dip in the lake or a quick cold rinse at home, if used every day as a routine you will feel more energetic and active. Above all the exposure of cold therapy will improve:

- sleep
- breath work
- skin elasticity
- aging
- stress release

- better immunity
- faster muscle recovery
- and prevent many other diseases

To receive the benefits of cold water therapy you can jump into a cold lake or swimming pool, take a cold shower for 2 minutes or ice bath, no longer than 10 to 15 minutes.

Water is life. Our bodies are 65% water. The Earth is covered with 65% water. The moon moves the water on the earth.

Find yourself near water as often as possible. Go to rushing rivers, bubbling streams, tumbling water falls, ocean waves, ponds, trickling fountains, swimming pools, hot springs and luxurious relaxing baths. Soak in the healing negative ions and enjoy the peaceful connection to divine feminine water.

**Shower Meditation:** Every time you take a shower, visualize washing away your stress and anxiety. Concentrate on the feel of the healing water upon your skin. Envision the power of the water washing away your negative thoughts. Feel sadness, regret, anger, self-doubt and depression washing right off you. Let it all go down the drain, you'll start to feel lighter and much more clear.

## Sun Bathing

The human race evolved under the sun, and the sun's healing powers have been worshiped for thousands of years.

Heliotherapy or sunbathing is one of the oldest ancient health care practices, used for thousands of years to keep people in a good level of health and to fight common illness by boosting immunity through the creation of natural unprocessed vitamin D. The first recorded information about this practice were found in ancient Greece, Egypt, Rome, Persia and even Babylon, which had sun-gardens. The physicians of the Roman time considered sun to be the best medicine and food in the world.

The introduction of Christianity put an end to the practice, for over a thousand years, as the Christians considered Heliotherapy as a sin.

From the late 1800s, heliotherapy became a very used technique in the treatment of tuberculosis of the bones, joints and skin. A long exposure to sunlight was proved to help in killing the bacteria which causes the disease.

Sunbathing for health is very, very different from sunbathing simply to get a tan. Exposure was very gradual, and only increased by about five minutes each day, starting with the feet and slowly working up the body. Sunlight early in the day had the greatest therapeutic value and sunbathing in cool conditions, at temperatures at or below 64° F, was considered particularly beneficial for patients with tuberculosis. This seems to have strengthened their immune systems and stimulated the self-healing powers of the body. Close attention was paid to the way each patient responded to the sun; and at the first sign of any reddening of the skin the treatment stopped. Nourishing meals were also part of the treatment. The proportion of fat in our diets, together with the mineral and vitamin content can influence the way our skin reacts to sunlight.

In his book, Human Culture and Cure, Dr G. D. Babbitt makes the following comment on the benefits of the sunlight: "There is a vast array of forces of every kind, including iron, magnesium, sodium, carbon and other elements conveyed by the sunlight, but why shall we not take these elements in their ordinary form from our drugstores, and not go to the trouble of taking sun-baths? Because when these elements are given to us in so refined a form, as to come directly from the sun as an ether, or to float skywards and be driven to us by the solar rays, they must be far more penetrating, enduring, safe, pleasant and up building to the mental system than if they were used in a crude form"

Sunlight brings life and warmth on Earth, we would not exist without it. From the perspective of Yin and Yang theory,

Sun offers yang energy, vitalizing our system. Most of the health challenges in our life are yin conditions. People who practice sunbathing have shown lowered blood pressure and cholesterol levels, regulated blood sugar and an increased white blood cell count. On the other hand, lack of sun exposure can lead to fertility problems, inflammatory bowel disease, heart disease, depression, cancer, arthritis.

Medical literature on heliotherapy is contradictory. While one field of investigation highlights the benefits, the other field presents it as a dangerous and health damaging practice.

What modern medicine does not understand is that exposure to sun does not cause cancer. The sunlight works as an accelerator. If you have a healthy diet, lifestyle, exposure to sunlight will accelerate your path towards longevity and health. If you have a toxic and additives based nutrition, exposure to sunlight will have an ill effect.

The sun-god Apollo was the Greek God of medicine and there are two inscriptions from his temple at Delphi that give, perhaps, the best advice on sunbathing to be found anywhere: "All things in moderation, Know thyself."

## Forest Bathing

Forest bathing is a simple process requiring you to take a few hours out of your day, occasionally, to go and wander in nature. It really is as easy as that.

To begin, head out towards a forest or woods and the rest is up to you. You could spend the time walking, resting or investigating plant life. Try to act on all of your senses, sight, smell, touch and hearing, enjoying a fully immersive experience of the forest. It doesn't matter if you don't get anywhere. You are not going anywhere. You are savoring the sounds, smells and sights of nature and letting the forest in.

A two-hour forest bath will help you to unplug from technology and slow down. It will bring you into the present moment and de-stress and relax you.

You can forest-bathe anywhere in the world, wherever there are trees; in hot weather or in cold; in rain, sunshine or snow. You don't even need a forest. Once you have learned how to do it, you can do shinrin-yoku (forest bathing) anywhere, in a nearby park or in your garden. Look for a place where there are trees, and off you go!

From FOREST BATHING: How Trees Can Help You Find Health and Happiness by Dr. Qing Li, published on April 17, 2018 by Viking, an imprint of Penguin Publishing Group, a division of Penguin Random House LLC. Copyright © Qing Li, 2018.

## Moon Bathing

Moonlight is the sun's light reflected off earth's lunar goddess. Its hue can be red-tinged, warm with sunset-streaked colors, or mysterious and vibey with violet undertones. No matter the time of year or the phase of the moon, the moon and the surrounding night darkness provides a cooling environment to offset hot summer days or stress-filled daytime interactions.

For millennia, the moon has been thought to hold a powerful influence over women, while in the traditional Indian medicine system of Ayurveda, moon bathing is used for calming Pitta Dosha (a fiery temperament or too much heat in the body). Today, with the artificial glare of light bulbs and that insidious blue glow from our smart phones, basking by the light of the moon has never seemed more attractive.

The moon's lunar energy brings the body's systems into harmony and promotes healing and wellness.

The lunar cycle is directly linked to earth's ocean tides, and throughout the entire history of humanity and across ancient and modern cultures, the moon has played a vitally important role in harvest, new beginnings, and decision making. The phases of the moon provide a time-marking cycle of 28 days, and the different moons are aligned with seasons in an intriguing way. With full moon names driven from ancient cultures, such as the Harvest Moon and the Wolf Moon, it's easy to see how the moon plays a major role in our lives.

Moon bathing is the natural activity for individuals who want to absorb the moon's energies and commune with nature in a way that does no harm, and does yourself a whole world of good. It doesn't even need to take place outdoors. All you need is a window to allow the moonlight to flood your space.

## Your Connection With the Moon

The ancients realized that everything on our planet depends on and is affected by the natural rhythms of our Moon. The phases of the moon influence the growth or decline of plants, animals, and human life. So basking in the moonlight was seen as a sacred and necessary part of every cycle.

I believe all women feel a special connection with the moon, I know I always have. It cycles just like we do and it's a bit more mysterious and reserved. It's soft while being extremely powerful, affecting our tides and all of nature.

- The New Moon (dark sky, no moon to be seen) is the time when you plant a new seed or intention.
- The Waxing Moon (the slim crescent moon which appears to grow larger each evening) is a time of taking inspired action.
- The Full Moon is a time to celebrate and feel gratitude for all that you've been given.
- The Waning Moon (a few days after the full moon it appears to get smaller each evening until it disappears)

reminds us to go back within to reflect and release what is no longer serving us so that we can prepare for the new cycle.

Those of us, who connect and walk with the ancients, and are drawn to the old ways; we feel the stars and moon deep within our bones.

## Healing Moon Meditation

The Healing Moon Meditation cleanses the mind of poisonous thoughts racing through a busy mind and clears toxic emotions stored in the heart. To start the meditation, you must reconnect with the moon. Each night, or as many nights a week as you can, gaze at the moon for five minutes. If you're not able to do it for that long, even doing it for 30 seconds will be helpful. You can first orient yourself to the wonder that is the moon and spend a moment appreciating it. It's helpful to generally be aware of the moon as much as possible. Know where it is and how it's magnetic force can help you heal and hold more light. As you stare at the moon for a few minutes or as long as you'd like, know that it is clearing your conscious of toxic thoughts, emotions, and stresses that are stored within us, influencing the decisions we make, the thoughts we think, and the feelings we experience. Toxic thoughts also affect our faith, trust, and compassion making it harder to navigate our way through life in a way that's in our best interests.

The moon doesn't have to be bright or full to do this meditation. You can sit or stand. All you need is to be able to see it and experience an intimacy with the moon for those few minutes. The moon has a magnetic frequency that gives it the amazing ability to draw out darkness for the time you do this meditation, giving you a fresh start instantly, even if you don't feel it yet yourself. Your soul starts to heal, your spirit starts to heal, and your heart starts to heal. Wounds you've collected from trust being broken, betrayal, or difficult situations you've had to bear, even illness or physical suffering, can start to mend. The more you do this meditation, the more profound its effects will be. Over time, you may feel yourself renewed and moving in a new and healthier direction. The Healing Moon Meditation is really that simple and that profound. It can be life-changing and it's right there for you every time you wish to use it.

There are many forms of meditation, each have their merits and can be helpful. If you are someone who struggles to meditate because it's hard to sit still, you don't have time, or you're in too much pain or too stressed to clear the thoughts from your mind, long sitting meditations may be too challenging for you. If that is the case this Healing Moon Meditation may be just what you need.

## Moon Energy Ceremony, any moon phase

Draw down the energy of the moon. You can do this exercise under the moon at any time in its cycle, the full & new moons are particularly potent. Plan to go outside and do this exercise at night.

Find somewhere you can stand in the light of the moon. Stand firmly grounded and hold your hands open above your head. Breathe Deep.

Ask for the divine light of the Feminine Moon to enter your hands and fill your body. Breathe in the light and the power of the moon. Allow it to fill your body; like a cup filled to the brim with light energy. Soak in the moon as long as you're able, then bring your hands to your heart. Say a soft prayer of thanks to the Mother Moon.

# Full Moon Ceremony

The moon receives its light from the sun shining it back to us with illumination. When the moon reaches its fullest, we often feel the pull of the sacred feminine. It is peak time for creative energy and intuitive breakthroughs. There's something activated within us, and our goddess connection calls for recognition. Get outside at night and let the light of the moon shine upon you. Just like our bodies need vitamin D from the sunlight we also benefit from moonlight. It is said to help reduce inflammation. Let her light nourish your soul.

There are so many ways that you can honor this inner divinity:

Gather all your crystals, divination tools, favorite jewelry and any other sacred items and take them outside for a moon bath. Depending on where you live and the current weather conditions, place them where they will not be damaged. A windowsill that gets direct moon light is perfectly fine if you can't get your items outside under the moon.

Take a few moments to reflect on what you are grateful for that has transpired in the past few weeks and take stock of what accomplishments you have made and the good things that have come to you that you have wished for or has brought joy or improvement to your life. Write them down on a piece of paper. The full moon represents fruitfulness and completion.

Also see if there is anything you are bumping up against to keep you from receiving the blessing or opportunities you desire in your life. Write down what is getting in the way of the experiences you have not received yet.

You can ceremonially burn the paper with these barriers or blocks, in a fire proof vessel or flush it down the toilet, or bury it, to release it to the universe.

What ritual wouldn't be complete without a bath? Water is symbolic of cleansing and recharging. Draw a hot bath and place any salts or oils you feel called to put in. Epsom salt is always a go-to of mine because it physically and energetically cleanses you. Light candles around your bath and turn out over-head lighting. Visualize this water recharging you after everything you've released tonight. Know that your path is cleared and you're ready to receive everything you've intended to receive.

## New Moon Journal Ceremony

The new moon and the week leading up the new moon is a magical time to spark new and exciting beginnings. It's a time to get clear about the things you really want to create and manifest into your life.

The New Moon brings us the energy of beginnings and is a cosmic refresher. It is a time to leave the past behind and immerse yourself in the energy of rebirth. Open yourself to abundance and possibility unfolding in your life.

If working with the elements, smudge the area. Visualize a circle of protective light around you. Light your candle, take a sip of your drink, and hold your crystals. You're shifting from a "doing" mode to a "being" mode so you can write in your journal from your true self, not the ego self that you identify with in your daily life.

This is the perfect time to declare to the Universe all the good things you wish to bring in your life. Write them all down in a New Moon Journal, no matter how crazy or big they may seem right now. What do you long for most? What does your heart desire? This is the time to dream big, so don't hold back, no matter how crazy or unrealistic your ideas may seem at the time.

On the bottom of your list, write, Universe, I ask for this or something better. I ask for the highest good of all involved. Thank you. I love you. I surrender these desires to you.

When you're done writing, close your journal, and say out loud, "So it is." Close the ritual with a prayer or a releasing meditation. Finish your tea, blow out your candle, and visualize the circle of light dissolving.

Trust that whatever happens, or doesn't happen, is for your highest good.

Don't get caught up in the need to control. Just surrender. In the days that follow, keep checking back on your list so you remember to take small, consistent action towards making your dreams a reality.

When an intention comes true, cross it off the list and thank the Universe for its deliverance.

Dedicate a "New Moon" journal for this practice. You can do this monthly with each new moon.


## Fire Ceremony

A fire ceremony is a traditional shamanic process that helps you to let go of things that are unhelpful in your life.

Fire is a great transmuter of energy, when we burn wood, oil, coal or candles, anything actually, it transmutes the energy of the fuel into heat, flame and smoke. The smoke rises up and drifts away. The native indigenous people use the fire to amplify the energy of your thoughts and intentions into spiritual vibration and send it into the universe via the medium of the rising smoke.

For them the ceremony of letting go, is a powerful one, their knowing is that the energy that made them heavy, or made them small or made them angry or sad, is changed forever by the fire and sent back to Source, no longer distorted by our human existence.

If you want to add another dimension to your fire ceremony choose a time of full moon or new moon building on the energy of the planets, but a fire ceremony can be held at any time, all you need is a flame and the feeling that you would like to bring change into your life.

You can use a fire pit or a fire bucket for safe burning. You can invite others to participate in the fire ceremony with you if you would like.

Write down everything you want to let go of, that no longer serves you, that you want to release as you move forward in your life. Set the intention to create some space in your mind, your energy and your life. Be still, sit with that intention, fold up your paper and throw it into the burning flame in the fire. Watch the flames consume it, follow the line of smoke up into the heavens.

Talk to the fire, tell it what it is you are letting go of. The vibration of your voice will intensify the energy. Watch the fire take your intention and transmute it to smoke that is carried up to the universe. Know that you have changed forever, creating space within you to attract something new, something that will help you in your quest for a life that you design.

Then write down everything you want to create in your life in the coming months, your dreams, abundance, everything you would like to manifest for your greater good.

Again, be still, sit with this intention, fold up your paper and burn it in the fire. Talk to the fire, asking it to bring that which you desire for your greater good, activating your abundance, again the vibration of your voice will intensify the energy, watch the fire take your intention up into the universe.

Allow the Universe to do its work. It has heard you. Make a commitment to the change you are calling in and take action towards your dreams, do it today, while the smoke of your fire ceremony still lingers in the air.

## Celebrate Seasonality as Our Ancestors Did

For as long as there has been humankind, there has been celebration. Whether it's the changing of the seasons or worshiping of some deity or idea, we'll always have a cause for revelry. When we have something to look forward to, or look ahead to something worth celebrating, we feel more optimistic. Celebrating the seasons, joy, love and being on this earth together is awesome and worth doing.

One of humanity's greatest advantages is our propensity for community, we can accomplish together what no one can pull off alone. It's not something that happens automatically or even all the time, of course, and we can be fractious. There are, though, two things that tend to bring us together: holidays and crises.

Our ancestors enjoyed holidays that celebrated shared joy at the completion of common tasks such as harvests, and reaffirmed their resolve to get through a hard winter together. Civilizations worldwide created rituals and celebrations to tip the balance into a fertile spring as their lives depended on the fertility of the earth. Going back to time immemorial we've come together for holidays that celebrate our commitment to one another in the face of both difficulties and achievements.

We can look to our ancestors, who planned their rituals to coincide with the changes in the season. They believed there was a direct relationship between the elements, the stars, and Spirit, who directed all things. Because they needed a way to predict and honor the seasons, they routinely celebrated moon cycles, the solstices (when the sun is at its greatest distance form the celestial equator and appears to stand still), and the equinoxes (when the sun crosses the plane of the earth's equator, making night and day of equal length all over the earth). Many people still live by these markers.

Those of us in the so-called modern world barely notice the seasons except to mark the beginning of a sport season or fashion collection. Thanks to technology, snow plows immediately clear the streets of snow, and air conditioners take the heat out of summer. Furthermore, most of us don't grow our own food; we opt for convenience, buying summer fruit in the middle of winter,

winter squash in May, and milk that comes from cartons rather than cows or goats. We rarely think about the significance of the seasons, whether plants are lying dormant or growing, whether animals are resting or bearing their young. In short, we have lost our intimate connection with the earth. Until recently, we hadn't even given much thought or energy to the precious resources we've wasted collectively as a species. (Earth Day, April 22, only dates back to 1970.)

Do you live someplace where you get to experience the full glory of all four seasons? If so, you know well the heady blossoms and dramatic skies of spring; the long, sun-drenched days of summer; the trees shaking in crimson and gold in fall; and the sparkling, brittle snows of winter.

As the world changes with each season everything is in flow. You can see a rhythm in the year that will never be explained by a calendar on the wall. With a new season every few months you start to see the connections between commonly celebrated religious festivals, like Christmas and Easter, and the distant past where these things actually mattered to the changing of the Earth. Careful attention to nature and an intention to connect to the natural world and connect to our ancestors is all that is needed to travel the depths of clarity with the seasons.

So why do I celebrate the seasons? They give me a peg on which to hang my moments of the year. They help me to remember to turn within, to reflect on all that has been and all that will come. The seasons are a practice in gratitude and awareness. The more I celebrate them the more I am aware of the world that is all around, of nature and her gifts, and how quickly times flies. It helps to keep things in perspective.

Make a toast, say a prayer, take a bite of a special food, sing a song, spend more time outdoors, light a candle. Animate the sweet moments with a powerful, celebratory action that fires up positive energy, and enjoy the goodness that you have in your life.

# Indulge Your Senses

*"Try to learn to breathe deeply, really taste food when*
*you eat, and when you sleep, really to sleep. Try as*
*much as possible to be wholly alive with all your*
*might, and when you laugh, laugh like hell. And when*
*you get angry, get good and angry. Try to be alive.*
*You will be dead soon enough." Ernest Hemingway*

The masculine largely gets lost in thought, while the feminine can get lost in the realm of the senses. Get out of your head, and into your body by intentionally living in your senses; sight, smell, touch, taste, sound.

**Sight**: The sense of sight has the strongest connection to our general state of mind. What we see has an impact on everything from creativity to our situational awareness.

A Norwegian study found that creating or consuming arts had positive benefits on physical health, personal satisfaction and lower rates of depression and anxiety.

Glistening water is always a mystical sight. Looking up at the moon is magical and romantic. The smiles on children's faces is innocence and love. Christmas trees and decorations make me happy.

**Smell**: Filling your home with the delicious aromas of cooking and baking is comforting and welcoming. Making perfumes, colognes and candles with essential oils is heavenly. Planting flowers in your garden is not only beautiful but smells delightful. The fragrance of fruit blossoms is euphoric. Planting an herb garden will delight your senses all summer long.

**Touch**: Indulge your sense of touch by going shopping and feeling all of the soft fabrics and fuzzy slippers. Feeling a soft breeze on your skin and tickling your hair is very pleasant. The sun on your skin is warm, healing and calming. Petting a dog or cat and running your fingers through their fur makes them roll over and beg for more. Pets are pure love.

People in society today have a need to be touched, but at the same time have almost a fear of being touched. We should all be hugged and kissed. A caring touch on our shoulder, arm or hand is very comforting. Holding hands makes you feel you belong to someone. Touch is one of those things that takes us right back to the womb. It connects us to one another.

**Taste:** Taste is the sense that registers the most pleasure for most people. Thousands of taste buds are stimulated from a myriad of flavors and combine with our scent receptors to give us the sensation of taste, from savory to sweet.

The five tastes; sweet, salty, sour, butter and umami (savory) are sensed by all parts of the mouth with certain areas having stronger reactions than others. A flavor is fully experienced only when all the taste buds have relayed the information to the brain.

To reconnect with your Divine Feminine Energy, occasionally indulge your taste buds by eating chocolate, drinking red wine, and indulging your palate with decadent foods that you love. You can also go to a public food market and take in all of the different sights and smells of the delicious food surrounding you.

**Sound:** Of the five senses, sound has the strongest link to how we perceive something and our emotions.

When you are walking on the beach and it's a sunny day and you feel good, you think it's because you're not at work. But really it's because you're grounding yourself. Your feet are in the sand and salt water and the minerals and negative ions are working on the body's electrical and chemical systems which helps balance your adrenals and thyroid.

Listening to the sound of waves crashing on the beach is my favorite. The sounds of running and trickling water is peaceful and life-giving. The sound of bees humming in my garden and birds singing in the trees is joyful and heartwarming. Hearing my chickens cackle when they lay their eggs always makes me chuckle. The wind rustling the leaves in the tall trees makes me feel so small, yet peaceful.

When we take time out of our busy schedules to focus on the senses we often take for granted, we enable ourselves to reap the benefits of some much needed relaxation and rejuvenation. So give yourself permission to re-wild yourself and enjoy some much needed "me" time with these tips for heightening your senses.

Once we experience the power of nature, we are reminded how important it is to work together to take care of this magical place that we call home, our Mother Earth!

# CHAPTER 8

## Ancient Tools for Healing Body, Mind and Spirit

*"Whenever you hear or read anything of a spiritual nature that moves you or touches your soul, you are not learning something, you are remembering what you have always known. It is a gentle awakening."*

We are born to be natural healers. Our bodies are made to heal themselves. Everything we need to heal is in nature and within ourselves. Somewhere in your past you knew the ancient ways. This is why you find yourself drawn to the wisdom of the natural world.

We live in a time with ancient wisdom at our fingertips and a multitude of ancient spiritual traditions from many cultures which are bursting forth in new forms for our Modern Age. We can bridge ancient beliefs and practices to match our modern sensibilities. I have included a few of these ancient tools for you to use to further cultivate your inner Goddess and heal the wounds of your body, mind and spirit. It is time to bring ancient wisdom alive and heal ourselves and our world.

The ancients just "knew" from experience their practices worked but in our modern world people want everything proven with science before they will consider its validity. Science is finally catching up with ancient wisdom and figuring out "how" the ancient practices work.

## Vibrational Energy

Science, through Quantum Physics, is showing us that everything in our universe is energy. Energy is created of light, color, sound, and vibration.

When we go down on a subatomic level we don't find matter, but pure energy. Some call this The Unified Field or The Matrix, others talk about Pure Potentiality, all being energy.

The universe is made up of different energies. Science shows us that everything is made up of energy. It's the building block of all matter. The same energy that composes your body is the same one that composes the bricks of the house you live in, your car, your phone, animals, trees and so forth. It's all the same energy vibrating at different frequencies.

We are all familiar with our physical bodies and their functions, but often less so with our bodies subtle energy systems. Seen from an energetic perspective each of us are made up of layers of vibrating energy, each of which has their own specific vibration and purpose.

Your vibration is your personal energy frequency. It is a culmination of every thought you have ever had and every action you have ever performed. It is the energy that surrounds and permeates every cell in your body.

Your vibration is your divine signature, your soul essence, and it is special only to you. Just as there are no two snowflakes alike, no two souls in the entire universe have the same name or "soul signature". That's how incredibly unique and special you are. Your vibration is a direct reflection of your inner thoughts, feelings, beliefs, choice of words, how well you take care of yourself, the earth and others.

**The higher your vibration the more light you hold, the faster your light particles vibrate, the higher your consciousness and the stronger you are connected to your soul. When you are a high vibrational being you recognize your divinity and the divinity within others. You are in alignment with your soul, which is nourished by spirit, you are vibrantly healthy and your life flows with ease and grace.**

Our aura is an electromagnetic field of energy that extends all around our body for about 4-5 feet. It radiates the health of our physical, mental, emotional, as well as spiritual energies, often including various colors.

**When your vibration is low, your light particles are vibrating slowly and become condensed. Your energy literally feels heavy because you are not in alignment with your soul or divine self and are mostly operating from your lower self or ego. Distorted beliefs, fear, anger, resentment, blame, guilt, jealousy, judgment, shame, addiction, un-forgiveness, conditional love, lack of self worth, greed, separation consciousness and poor health keep you in very dense low vibrating energy.**

Finally, when we increase our vibrational frequency, we are honoring the divine within us, the connection to ourselves, our core, our truth, and also something bigger than us, honoring the belief we are here on this earth for a reason living out our divine plan.

When we feel connected to ourselves and something bigger than us, we can operate from a place of divine love and know that everything is okay and as it should be in the world. We know that we do matter and that we have an important purpose here, and it's then that we are more likely to choose the foods, activities and people that truly nourish our soul.

# Energy Work

Energy healing is one of the oldest practices in the world today.

Energy work is a form of alternative medicine that relies on the idea that the body is filled with and surrounded by energy fields that can be manipulated. Energy work takes a wide variety of forms, and is offered from practitioners in many areas of the world. According to energy workers, the health of the human body and mind rely on stability in the energy fields in and around the body.

Any healing technique which deals only with the physical body and the energy field of the individual tends to accomplish one thing: it jump starts the individual, so to speak, and gives him or her an added boost of energy. That energy boost then allows that person's own internal healing mechanism to become mobilized into greater activity.

There are hundreds of types of energy healing methods, including Polarity Therapy, Qigong, Chakra Balancing, Reiki and Shiatsu. Other holistic methods of energy healing include acupuncture, acupressure, and even crystal healing.

There are many wonderful energy healing modalities. Below I will touch on only a few that came from our ancient ancestors.

# Intention

The ancients, shamans, yogis, and sages have all understood the power of intention. Now new scientific discoveries about the biochemical effects of the brain's functioning show that all the cells of your body are affected by your thoughts. The new science of epigenetics is revolutionizing our understanding of the link between mind and matter.

Intentions are the fuel to manifesting your goals and visions. An intention will help create more clarity in your life.

Crafting powerful intentions starts by setting goals that align with your life's values, aspirations, and purpose. Your chosen intention should always be positive, uplifting, and always in the present tense. You want to refrain from using any negative words.

When we use energy for healing, amazing things happen. Because it is a living form of consciousness, energy is intelligent and already knows where to go and what to do.

When we add an intention to that energy, the intention directs the energy specifically, based upon our intention. The energy gains purpose instead of being just a broad wave of energy that we sent without intention. Like a laser beam, intention directs energy to a specific goal or target.

When we add passion or emotion to an intention the passion acts as fuel to power the energy toward a directed cause.

Your body believes everything your mind tells it. The powerful energy of intention can move energy in the body, change cells and genes and bring forth healing. **Where attention goes, energy flows.**

As with all spiritual things, the most important points are to ask for what you need (set your intention) and trust that it will be given to you. Your Spiritual Guides are just waiting to help you.

## Meditation

> "Meditation is about letting go, being open, and being curious enough to seek out the divine, without any expectations or forcing outcomes." Dr. Joe Dispenza

Meditation is when you connect with your Higher Self (soul) and your Spirit team intentionally by entering a "witness" state of mind. When you meditate, you mentally leave the physical world and connect with yourself and your purpose.

The reason we focus on our breathing so heavily when we meditate is that it is one of the actions that can be controlled by both the conscious and subconscious minds.

As we relax more deeply we become a mix of subconscious and conscious, until eventually both are united and transcend to a state of super-consciousness. It is during this process that we can very easily release old paradigms and install new ones. Simply visualize your intent while you meditate. This is rewriting your subconscious. All a personal paradigm really is, is a story that we keep subconsciously telling ourselves until it becomes real around us. Now is the time to write a new story with a happier ending.

## Hypnotherapy

Hypnotherapy is modern psychology's version of guided meditation to reach your subconscious. Hypnosis works very similar to meditation, the only difference and benefit being that there is someone to guide you every step of the way.

Many people find that meditation and visualization do not work for them because they get distracted, their phone starts buzzing, or they just can not figure out how to be both relaxed and invested at the same time. A good hypnotherapist can assist in all of those things.

More likely than not he or she will have you turn your phone off on the outset of the session. Their voice and instruction that are both calm but authoritative will keep you focused, and the fact that you probably paid money to have this session take place will make you much more invested in focusing.

He or she will teach you how to relax and have an environment that you may feel more suited to this work than your own home.

# Pendulums

I use pendulums as a healing tool with great success and have taught many clients how to use them at home for themselves and their families. I have encountered some religious people who are very fearful of them and think they are evil. So I have included the history of pendulums and you can decide for yourself if it is something you may want to consider trying.

Pendulum dowsing history is a long and varied one. Pendulums are also commonly known as dowsers, and people have used them for thousands of years throughout history. Historically, pendulums are widely known for their use in locating water, oil, iron, and even for mining silver and gold. Dowsing rods are possibly used more commonly for this type of finding, but the principle is the same.

2200BC: The Chinese Emperor Yu, who was an explorer and dowser, believed to have found geopathic stress zones through dowsing and left written decrees forbidding any building of homes on these areas when he sailed ships to Western America and the Mexican coasts.

Dowsing is mentioned in the Bible, too. And is known to have been used by the Greeks, Romans, Celtic Druids as well as the ancient Chinese.

1300BC: In the Old Testament, a Rod was used by Moses and Aaron to find water in the desert, along with Egyptians Hieroglyphs, describing a magician's wand or rod. This wand was called Ur-Heka, and its meaning translates to "Great magical power."

47BC: Cleopatra was said to have carried dowsers with her always and used them to find gold.

1271AD: Marco Polo knew of pendulums, dowsing rods, and the compass, all of which he learned from the Chinese between 1271-1295. He used them all widely.

1478-1834AD: Spanish Inquisition. Possibly one the most known and widely recognized times in history regarding pendulum dowsing. The inquisition attempted to banish all religions that followed the Goddess and stop women's Psychic or Healing abilities.

At this time, people considered dowsing to be evidence of witchcraft, and approximately 9 million people were burned at the stake or hung during the years of the inquisition. Most of them tortured before their death, and nearly all of them were women and girls. They were Psychics, Healers, Midwives, Dowsers, Goddess worshipers, and Herbalists. This continued for many years throughout history.

1518AD: Martin Luther, the German Monk, University Professor, Theologian, Priest, and founder of Protestantism, proclaimed that the use of dowsing rods was a violation of the first commandment. He quoted, "Thou shalt have no other Gods before me," which is one of the ten commandments. Even though pendulums and rods were not worshiped but used as a tool.

1558-1603AD: Queen Elizabeth I, introduced dowsing to England in the 16th century to keep up with the success that Germany had experienced. She used dowsing for mineral location in Cornwall. By 1600AD, dowsing was a common practice for mining throughout Europe.

1563-1763AD: The persecution of witches in England. Another lengthy period in history and went on throughout the time of the Spanish Inquisition. That continued for approximately 200 years and is commonly known as "the burning times." However, the abolishment of England's anti-witchcraft laws was not until 1951.

1627AD: Martine de Bertereau and her husband, Jean de Chatelet, both from France, were both arrested and sentenced to life in prison for dealings in witchcraft. The highly skilled dowser Martine used her skills to find more than 150 coal mines of which were profitable. Both the Baron and Baroness were later released, but they had all of their equipment confiscated.

Martine was a mining engineer and became a mining adviser for the French government and discovered the now-famous tourist attraction Chateau Thierry mineral springs in 1629. She wrote a book on dowsing in 1640 and was rearrested with her husband again for the partaking in witchcraft. Jean and Martine both died in separate prisons.

1701AD: Dowsing in France for tracking criminals was prohibited by 1701, and at this time, Pendulum Dowsing was common practice rather than the use of dowsing rods.

1800's: Around this time, Pendulums and dowsing went into a decline. That was due to insufficient evidence on how or why dowsing was so accurate in this age of reason. Many historical figures were interested in dowsing: The likes of Albert Einstein was a dowser himself and predicted that one-day science would be able to give explanations of this phenomenon.

Other famous and widely known figures, all of which scientists that had dealings with pendulum dowsing were, Sir Isaac Newton, Leonardo Da Vinci, and Thomas Edison.

More Recently: During the 1920s saw the revival of pendulums and dowsing techniques throughout England. Pendulums came into widespread use as a medical diagnostics tool. In France, more than 2,500 medical professionals used pendulums for diagnostic use, and this continued until after WW2.

Armies worldwide have used pendulums and dowsing. General George Patton of WW2 employed dowsers, as did Robert McNamara, the secretary of state, during the Vietnam war to locate land mines, underground tunnels, and ammunition dumps. Soviet geologists had also revived pendulum dowsing in the 1960s as a successful experiment with mining.

In modern-day technology, dowsers still have their place. Water companies still use them to locate new water sources. Oil companies, as well as mining industries, still use this technology, and they believe that pendulum dowsing use will continue in this way for many years to come.

Some other official names who are supportive of pendulum dowsing include: The British Army, The British Academy of science, The US Marines, The Academy of Sciences of Paris, The United Nations Education, NASA. The former Soviet Union and many, many more.

## What is a Pendulum?

A pendulum is a weight on the end of a string, thread or chain. When hanging from your fingers your own vibrational energy moves the pendulum to swing one way or the other. When you ask a yes or no question, your positive or negative energy, or the earths vibrational energy will swing the pendulum in a yes or no direction.

## Using Pendulums for Healing

A pendulum can be used as a training tool to communicate with your subconscious, much like muscle testing. Pendulums are tools that can help you to understand your subconscious mind on a conscious level. All the magic is within you, and pendulums just help you to manifest it more easily.

So, when you use a pendulum, you or the earths energy are moving it unconsciously. Spirits do not move the pendulum for you. It is a spiritual thing but not a 'paranormal' thing, like a ouija board. They are not evil and there is no witchcraft involved. However I am still amazed at how many people still believe they are "bad" and won't have anything to do with them, not realizing their fear comes from the first church fathers lies to take away personal power.

I have used pendulums for healing for years to help my clients discover foods they are intolerant to, the best nutritional supplements for them and therapeutic doses their body needs for healing, etc.

I love my pendulums for the aid and confidence they can give us for our own self healing. I love and appreciate them even more after researching their persecutors deceptive history!

**Choosing Your Pendulum:** You can purchase a pendulum in shops or online. They may be made from crystals, glass, wood, stones or metal. I have several pendulums that I just couldn't resist when I saw them. They are different designs, gemstones and sizes. The important thing is that you are drawn to it and it is comfortable in your hands. Choosing a pendulum, whether you want one or many is a personal matter.

If you are interested in learning how to use a pendulum you should seek out a practitioner or energy worker and see how they use it. There are also a few pendulum books I recommend in the reference section.

### You Can Use Your Body as a Pendulum

Using our bodies puts us much more closely in tune with our being. The process of using your body as a pendulum is to ask your higher self a question and wait for your body to respond in either a forward-tilting or backward-tilting motion. The first step is to really understand how your higher self communicates with you by centering your body, asking yourself the directions for "yes" and "no," and noting which way your body moves. For a lot of people a forward motion is "yes," and your body tilting backward is a "no" answer. It is easier to start with simple questions at first to understand how your higher self communicates with you. As you become more used to the messages you receive and how you process them, you can start asking for more specific things such as what dosage of herbs or vitamins to take or which foods would best nourish your body. Using this technique in the grocery store or when shopping for vitamins and remedies can be extremely helpful.

Since we are always present in our bodies, understanding how we can use our bodies as pendulums is a tool we can use at any given moment in our lives.

## Color Therapy

Color and light have been used for healing since the beginning of recorded time. Hippocrates observed the effect color has on the healing process. Ancient Egyptians built solarium-type rooms with colored panes of glass. The sun would shine through the glass and flood the patient with color. Some people placed colored silk cloths on their body and then flooded with sunlight.

During the Middle Ages, everything that was regarded as 'pagan' was exorcized, including healing with color.

The Persian physician Avicenna continued the art of color healing. He stressed the importance of using color both in diagnosis and treatment of dis-ease or illness.

Paracelsus, a Swiss doctor, resurrected the healing arts during the Renaissance in Europe. To him, light and color were vital for good health. He used elixirs, charms and talismans, and herbs to treat people.

Color works through and in us, in every nerve, cell, gland and muscle. It shines in our auras and radiates upon us from the sun. Color is an active power, exerting a tremendous influence on our consciousness and soul.

Each color of the rainbow has its own frequency, power and vibration. A study published by the National Institutes of Health, saw significant improved skin complexion and feeling through light therapy.

Researchers have discovered that everything on this planet depends on light for survival. What's even more interesting, is that researchers have now discovered that our every cell is capable of emitting light. When you consider this in line with the concept of the aura, it makes sense that some people with unique abilities might be able to sense this interesting phenomena.

We know that when all colors join the result is white light. Therefore working with White Light brings about completeness, oneness, union of all complementary parts.

Color vibrations bypass human reasoning to work at the cellular level. Colors are a conduit for positive energy shifts, and serve as a powerful path for healing and recovery. Specific colors have vibrational properties that speed up, balance, or calm down thinking and behavior.

Scientists have shown that color affects our psychological disposition of mood, energy, feelings and behavior. Studies have proven that the color red will increase heartbeat, blood pressure and body temperature and that people who have the same illness avoid the same color.

Take a look at the colors you surround yourself with, the colors you wear, the colors you feel drawn to, and the colors you love. Are they similar shades? Focus on bringing color into your life for a purpose, and you are sure to discover new ways to increase your health and well-being.

## Moon Phases

The New Moon is the beginning phase of the moon, when the light of the moon is not visible from Earth. This is because the side of the moon that is illuminated by the Sun, is not facing Earth. New Moons are a time of new beginnings and they represent the youthful aspect of the Goddess, bringing youth, change and a fresh start. New Moons are great times to set intentions, move, or start new projects, new careers, relationships, or any new venture in life. Whatever you decide to do during the New Moon, know that this is a time of cosmic reset and rebirth. Take the time you need to rest, replenish, go within, rework your goals, dream your dreams for the future and tap into the hope that anything is possible.

The Full Moon is a time of great power since the moon is at the height of its strength, marking a fullness of metaphysical power. This is the time to do any work that involves reaching its fullest potential, growth or celebration of abundance. The full moon represents the mature or mother aspect of the Goddess embracing wisdom, maturity, nourishment, creativity, and fertility. This is an excellent time for protection and divination.

The illumination of the Full Moon is a time of recharging and restoring energy to crystals, art and healing tools. Some crystals are sensitive to sunlight, so a better way to charge and clear them is in the light of the Full Moon. This can be done directly outside or in a window sill. A simple charging for these items is to place them where they will be bathed in the Full Moon light, offer your intentions (pure creative potential, divine inspiration, sight into the sacred, a channel of truth, etc) and offer a blessing of thanks for the energy and illumination that is being imbued by the Mother Moon.

The Dark Moon appears totally dark in the sky or it may seem that there is no moon out at night. It occurs 3 days prior to the New Moon. This is the time for introspection and contemplation, for rest, for quiet, and for inward focus. The Dark Moon is also a time of healing. The Dark Moon provides us with the opportunity to leave behind anything from the past that is no longer needed. This is the time to prepare for new growth in the coming lunar cycle.

## Labyrinths

A labyrinth is an ancient spiritual tool for prayer, meditation and heightened awareness. To build a labyrinth is to create sacred space, and to walk a labyrinth is to imbue it with power and meaning. The more a labyrinth is used, the more powerful it can become as a symbol of transformation.

Drawings on rock art located in areas of Nevada, Cornwall, Lancashire, and Spain, are estimated to date back as far as 10,500-4800 BCE.

Labyrinth patterns are universal, being found as archaic petroglyphs, Amerindian basket weaving designs, and paintings and drawings from all over the word. Variations of the seven-circuit labyrinth have been found worldwide, from Peru to Arizona. Iceland, Scandinavia, Crete, Egypt, India and Sumatra.

Labyrinths are ancient patterns found all over the world. Their origin is as mysterious as their uses and as varied as their patterns are. A labyrinth is a complex and circuitous path that leads from the beginning point to the center. The path twists and turns back on itself many times before reaching the center. A meander with a single, undivided path and no choices to make other than traveling onward through the winding pattern to an assured goal.

The seven circuits of the Labyrinth correspond with the seven spheres of the sacred planets of the human being and the cosmos, the seven days of the week, and other such sevenfold meanings. Passing to the center of the labyrinth and returning to its circumference represents the involution and evolution of the universe, the coming into birth and the passing out of the earthly life of an individual, and most important a journey into the center of our own being, the achievement of a quest for wholeness, and the subsequent return to our divine source.

The winding pattern of any labyrinth also represents the circulation of vital energies within our bodies, and that pattern suggests the convolution of the brain and the intestines, two poles of our body corresponding to our consciousness and its physical vehicle. To traverse the labyrinth is to bring into one wholeness all parts of our being.

Labyrinths go back almost 5,000 years, long before Christianity. As with many pre-Christian symbols, the labyrinth was converted for Christian use. As a result, church labyrinths have developed a specifically Christian tradition that dates back to the middle ages. The famous labyrinth at Chartres Cathedral in France dates back to the early 13th century and was walked by pilgrims as part of their pilgrimage.

How to Walk a Labyrinth: To walk a labyrinth enter and follow the path to the center, where you may wish to pause for a few moments. You then reverse your direction and retrace your path back out to the starting point. In walking any labyrinth, you should always complete the pattern by following the pattern inward and outward, rather than cutting across the pattern at any point. The inward movement needs to be complemented by a corresponding outward return.

If several people walk the labyrinth together, they may pass one another, either going in the same direction or opposite to each other. They may pass in meditative silence or quietly salute each other by a nod of the head or a raising of the hands. You do not need to be somber around it, but if someone is walking the labyrinth, it is courteous to respect the need they may have for quiet concentration.

As you enter the labyrinth you may focus on a question or concern or with a quiet meditative mind. There is no single right way to walk the path. Walking the labyrinth is surprisingly calming and clarifying for your thoughts. Even if you don't have a spiritual side, the slow intentional walking in a quiet place on a set path allows for a level of focus that can be difficult to find in a busy life.

I love labyrinths. I have walked them in prayer, meditation, with a particular intention, and also combining the walk with a fire ceremony in the center, to release things that no longer serve me.

Labyrinths are usually found on church grounds and spiritual retreat centers. The World-Wide Labyrinth Locator allows you to search by country, city, state, and zip code. The listings include descriptions, directions, open hours and photos.

You can create your own temporary labyrinth by using a basic pattern and laying out stones, sticks or drawing it in the sand. More permanent labyrinths are created with garden paths, plantings and rock work.

## Medicine Wheels

For many modern people, medicine is associated with drugs, surgical procedures, nurses, dentists, or doctors that all improve one's physical health. However, "medicine" in many past ancient cultures was understood as an interrelated process of physical and spiritual well-being. Medicine was once thought of as a way of being in harmony with the primal energy of nature, and a way of becoming aware of the personal power within each of us that allows us to become more whole and complete.

A Medicine Wheel is a ceremonial tool used by many spiritual people all over the world to perform rituals that honor the four directions, the sacred hoop of life, the animals, the sun, moon, Mother Earth, Father Sky, and many more aspects of the natural world.

"Medicine" is anything that deepens your relationship with the Creator and the Great Spirit and brings you closer to harmony and balance.

The wheel is made up of a circle divided into four directions, the east, south, west and north. Also a symbol of astrology, each person is represented somewhere within that circle depending upon their birth month and day. That placement is associated with a special moon, power animal, totem clan, healing plant, color and mineral.

Today, Medicine Wheel ceremonies are becoming more popular and can be found all over the world. As the teachings spread to different cultures, it is a bit modified, therefore not every ceremony will be alike.

## Women's Circles

*"Part of healing the wounded feminine and*
*reclaiming feminine wisdom is for the women*
*to reconnect, to come together as sisters with a*

*common mission rather than stay isolated and*
*reinforce a divisiveness which disempowers us all*
*and weakens our efforts" Jane Hardwicke Collings*

Finding or building a community of like-minded women can really help to strengthen your relationship with feminine energy. I have found that attending or creating women's circles can help to build this type of supportive and loving community. It can also be very healing to communicate and share the things that are happening in your life with other women. The feeling of sisterhood with other women is incredibly healing, there is no doubt about that!

Now is the time for women to come together and support each other. The time of jealousy, competition, and rivalry amongst women needs to come to an end and is coming to an end with our help.

There is evidence of spiritual ritual gatherings occurring possibly as early as 300,000 years ago in Middle Paleolithic societies, although little is known about the complexity of these gatherings. Actual evidence is found that communities gathering for spiritual and shamanic experience have been evidenced in the Upper Paleolithic societies, long before modern humanity. Although there is no written history, there is evidence of ritual art, paint, and other religious ceremonial relics, including the first representations of the revered female form. This means that human beings have been gathering in purposeful circle for a very long time, and that the central representation of divinity was feminine.

Women equally participated in circles around the fire for ritual and did the same as they prepared food for families and community. During these times they shared stories and tribal experience.

In many ancient cultures, women would retreat away from society during their "Moon cycle" which coincided with the occurrence of the New Moon. In some cultures, women would gather voluntarily in Moon lodges during their cycle to nest, embrace womanhood, and enhance their mental, physical and spiritual health. A time to share stories, rest, heal, nurture their bodies and the sacred bond of womanhood. Moon lodges or red tents as they are commonly referred to, were a safe space for girls to become women. As many may forget, like clockwork our usual cycle is almost perfectly in sync with the Moon. Upon their first period, girls were invited into the red tent society to learn from the generations that preceded them how to take care of their cyclic nature as a woman.

Ancient rituals included bleeding into mother earth as an offering, chanting, adorning in red, face and body paint, womb massage, indulging in sweets, creating a sacred altar and telling stories of warrior women and goddesses.

So what happened between then and now to make women's circles all but disappear from conventional culture? We weren't allowed to come together because it made people feel uncomfortable, and we were persecuted for it.

In 1484, the *Hammer of Witches* publication by two German Dominican monks began the systematic destruction of women's spiritual practices and health care by torturing and murdering women healers and spiritual leaders. This oppression lasted 500 years and was carried with colonialism to every corner of the Earth.

That didn't completely stop women from getting together on their own terms, from sewing and quilting circles to tea dates and Mary Kay parties. We were still called to gather, but we weren't allowed to dip into an energy that would offend the power of the masculine.

Women are awakening. We're remembering our roots. A remembrance that runs through our blood. This is why when we gather in circle it feels like coming home. Your blood remembers.

In circle we are all equal. No one is above another. You realize that you are not alone with what you're experiencing in life.

Everyone is going through something. You see yourself in your sisters stories. In their pain, realness, triumphs and tears. You realize that no one has it all together and that life is messy and complicated. And that's OK.

Stepping into circle feels completely natural. That's because coming together in circle is completely natural. It's gaining more popularity nowadays but this isn't something new. Women have been gathering in circles for thousands of years.

There is a lot of shame, guilt, and stigma around sharing deep thoughts and emotions. This needs to be normalized in order to stimulate the feminine consciousness, which is what the world needs. Empathy, kindness, compassion, non-judgment, nurturing interactions, openness, creativity, and softness comes with strong Feminine Energy.

At first it can feel vulnerable to let your guard down and step into circle. The mistrust among women runs deep. For generations women have been pinned against each other. We have seen each other as our competition. We have been taught to gossip, judge, and put each other down.

In the Circle, we are all equal. There is no one in front of you and there's nobody behind you. No one is above you; no one is below you. The Circle is Sacred because it is designed to create Unity.

Psychologists have proven that endorphins (the hormone of love and well-being) are released into our brains when we talk about ourselves. Some say that's one of the many benefits of therapy. In our women's circle, we start with a "Check-In", where each woman gets 10 minutes to be fully heard by the group. She can use this time to talk about anything on her mind.

The rest of the women give their full and raptured attention without interruption. To be heard by a group of people who you know love you deeply, feels absolutely glorious. Women can share freely without fear of judgment, in an environment that feels completely safe and supported. Practicing the art of listening deeply also gives us a chance to tap into our empathy and patience, keeping us present in the moment without thinking about how we will respond.

Sharing your experiences with others can yield powerful revelations. Seeing friends deal with the same life challenges you have, makes you realize you are not the only person with these problems. We all have times of low self-esteem, conflicts at work or in our relationships, of feeling challenged by parenting, money, or health.

When we meet in circle we join to hold everyone in sacred space and purpose. We are bringing forth an ancient way of connecting into modern times. We gather to share stories, to deepen our identities individually and in group, often with the intention to enable and shape a post-patriarchal way of being. We also gather to heal. We can meet in circle to share our joy, we can meet in circle to work on projects or join in ritual at various levels of depth and purpose, and we can meet in circle to help to change our world.

When we see each other transform our life challenges into opportunities, we feel stronger than ever. We are reminded that we can do the same. When we are stuck in our own problems, it can be difficult to see the light at the end of the tunnel.

Sometimes it takes a sounding board to bring the resonance of your own inner wisdom to the foreground, with the presence of others to amplify your inner light as you allow each other to shine.

There are many kinds of circles depending on the needs of the members, they can be support circles, healing and wellness circles, spirituality circles, or action circles. In Native American women's circles, there was a talking stick and storytelling, a lot of sharing and listening. Per Jewish tradition, the circle is open lighting a candle and asking everyone to state her mother's and grandmothers' names. A Shamanic circle may involve drumming and journeying. Others may incorporate yoga, meditation, singing, moon rituals, astrology, oracle card readings, etc.

Regardless of the style, the main purpose of a women's circle is to bond in sisterhood. Many women experience loneliness, depression and anxiety. Joining a women's circle that you relate to will change your life. You will find friends, acceptance and non-judgement. This kind of connection and community is incredibly healing.

# CHAPTER 9

## Find Your Roots

Humans are historically tribal people and live in community. It is only in recent years that we have had the ability and opportunity to easily move across the country and travel the world, sometimes settling far from home. Many of us grow up without extended family members nearby and are disconnected from our tribe, and don't participate in cultural ceremonies or learn the stories of our ancestors.

## Your Heritage

Everyone is indigenous to somewhere. We all have roots to the land, a land where our divine grandmother's lived and their stories where told. A land where our ancient ancestors land was taken over. Every indigenous culture has had someone come in and steel their land, their women and children, their way of life, their resources, traditions and beliefs. They were either stolen, displaced or migrated from their original homeland.

Some of us are only a few generations away from our great grandmothers who still told the stories and knew the ways of their ancestors and still carry generational emotional wounds in their subconscious. Some of us still have a pure enough bloodline to look like our ancient ancestors but most of us are far removed from our roots and consciousness of our divine feminine great, great, great grandmothers and who they were, they are no longer remembered or talked about.

Some of our parents and grandparents before them have traveled and moved to far away lands and intermarried time after time, leaving us with no particular identity, culture, tribe or traditions to hold on to. Our roots may be scattered in many lands leaving us feeling disconnected and not belonging to anyone or any place. We see our friends and acquaintances who have rich cultural backgrounds and who are still connected to their cultural traditions and language, this can leave us with an emptiness and longing to know who our ancestors were and where we came from.

In order to know who you are, and where you fit into the world, you need to know where you came from.

Knowing which countries your ancestors came from may help you feel more grounded and connected to the people who live in that country today and who may be in dire situations. Knowing your family history can help you find common ground with people who lived long ago and today.

## DNA Testing for Your Ethnic Origin

DNA test results give you a vivid look into your genetic history, from recent to ancient ancestry. It does this by closely looking at your personal DNA, and allowing you to see the molecular components that make you, you.

An ancestry DNA test can analyze millions of separate data points on the human genome. Since humans have about 99.9% of their DNA in common, the point is to take a close look at the specific genetic markers that vary from one another and make us each unique.

The analysis of these differentiating markers can provide a very accurate indication of who your ancestors were. If your markers are similar to those of a particular group, then you've most likely descended from that group.

Don't worry if your DNA test results say that you're part Neanderthal, it doesn't mean anything bad.

Neanderthals were just one of many human species that existed 40,000 years ago. They lived in Europe and then, for reasons unknown, died off before civilization began. However, they mingled with other human species while they were around. So, it's typical for anyone with European ancestry to have a bit of Neanderthal in their DNA.

Finding the right DNA test kit really depends on your specific needs. So you have to have a good idea of what you're in the market for. No two vendors are exactly the same. Some companies can even tell you the migration history of your family and others specialize in coupling your test results with access to billions of historical records to help build your family tree. On the other hand, while a vendor might not offer that wealth of information, it may offer a decently detailed ancestry report at a very cheap price.

## Genealogy and Family History

When people start searching for information about their ancestors, they often begin by looking for vital records and filling in their family tree. Your family tree can show you exactly how you are related to all of your ancestors.

Not all genealogists take the time to also become family historians, but this is where the gold is. Your family history helps to provide meaningful connections to your ancestors. Old photos, letters, and journals give you a glimpse into what your ancestors were really like. Stories handed down from one generation to the next about something an ancestor did can be inspiring. Family history is what makes a name and series of dates on a page into a living, breathing, person.

Digging into genealogy and family history can fulfill a desire to pass on a legacy to future generations and allow families that have migrated from another country the opportunity to preserve some of the culture of their old country.

Genealogy is one of the fastest growing hobbies in the western world, as more and more people discover the exhilarating and slightly addictive nature of ancestor hunting. It's like an ongoing mystery with clues you have to discover and then put together to come to conclusions about your family's past. The mystery never ends, because there is no end to the amount of time you can potentially go back in history with your family research. Yet, the more you can discover, the more complete picture of your family you can put together. It's insanely rewarding, and the more you do it, the more you will want to do it.

When you're out in the field doing genealogy, you can get in touch with your ancestors in a way you never would imagine. You actually start to see them as real, once living people, not just names on a sheet of paper or computer program. It is actually possible to develop relationships with your ancestors the more you get to know them, and you get a better idea of who you are and where you came from by getting close to the ancestors who are responsible for making you. The more you discover about them, the more people you have in your life to love. You really can start to love those ancestors, and you will be surprised at the close relationships you develop with some of them, you will be naturally drawn to some more than others.

Out in the field, you really get an idea of how your ancestors lived. You will go to the towns (often still very small and rural) where they lived, look at old maps to discover where their homesteads were (and sometimes discover they are still there), visit the cemeteries where they and their immediate relatives are buried, and discover old documents they signed and be amazed that you're touching something they touched.

You will naturally meet some living relatives in the course of your research who you never knew existed before you started your search. The process of seeing just how you are connected is exciting in itself, as you see the generations tangle as they move out from your common ancestor and into the present day. Many of these people will have (or will know people who have) information, documents, and even photos to help and add to your ancestor research that you couldn't have found any other way.

By doing this work you are honoring your ancestors by bringing them back into the light and putting the details of their lives back together. Remember, these were living people once, real people who actually walked the earth. They deserve to be remembered by their descendants, just as you would want to be remembered. In a very real way, you are doing a service to them by pulling them out of the obscurity of time and back into the present to re-introduce them to the many descendants they produced.

Your ancestors are not lost, everything is remembered on a spiritual level, which you have access to.

*"Walking. I am listening to a deeper way. Suddenly all my ancestors are behind me. Be still they say. Watch and listen. You are the result of a thousand loves." Linda Hogan*
**Native American Writer**

# CHAPTER 10

## How Divine Feminine Energy Will Bring Corrective Balance to the World

*"The world will be saved by the western woman."*
**Dalai Lama**

Our ancient ancestors spent most of their time outdoors. They walked on the earth, worked under the sun, rested under the shade of trees, grew food in the soil, bathed in the oceans and rivers, gazed at the stars and moon at night and worked together as a community for their survival. They lived with the cycles of the moon and the seasons. They slept when it was dark and arose with the sun in the morning. They knew they were not alone, that there is life after life, and ways to communicate with the spirit world.

I am in awe and feel very connected to the ancients when I think how we walk on the same earth, live under the same sun, moon and stars, drink, bathe and fish the same rivers they did. We feel the same cool breezes on our skin, warmed by the same sun, hear the same ocean waves and experience the changing of the seasons as they did.

Before we are born the first vibration we feel is our mother's blood running through her arteries and veins. We vibrate to that primordial rhythm even before we have ears to hear. The first sound we hear is our mother's heartbeat. Before we were conceived, we existed in part as an egg in our mother's ovary. All the eggs a woman will ever carry form in her ovaries while she is a four-month old fetus in the womb of her mother. This means our cellular life as an egg began in our grandmother's womb. Each of us spent five months in our grandmother's womb and she in turn formed in the womb of her grandmother. We vibrate to the rhythms of our mother's blood before she herself was born. And this pulse is the thread of blood that runs all the way back through the grandmothers to the first mother. We all share the blood of the first mother. We truly are children of one blood.

Much love and sharing is needed to awaken us all to the chaos we are creating and living in, and guide us back to our true nature as divine beings living on earth.

We know the feminine has been suppressed for the past few thousand years, but although she has been pushed down and hidden, she has not been destroyed. She can never be destroyed. She is still within you, as she is within me, and every being on the planet.

Regardless of what is going on around us, we have the power to embrace and express the Divine Feminine within us. We can act with compassion, promote peace, live in abundance, nurture ourselves and our earth, and slow down so we can live a richer, fuller life.

The Divine Feminine will rescue our planet, returning light and harmony to it. But we have to awaken her within ourselves first. With Divine Feminine Energy we will work together as one to reshape the world. We need to lead like women, not be bad clones of men, and our Divine Feminine traits are the pathway to bring balance to the world.

**The Divine Feminine woman is:**

- Confident and doesn't need validation from others.
- She embraces her age, color, shape and size and honors her divinity.
- She is able to balance her ability to listen and nurture with her ability to drive and control.
- She is able to lead with authority, and at the same time show her vulnerability.
- She cares for people as much as she cares about profits.

That return and strength of Divine Feminine Energy is what is causing huge disruption to our world; a breakdown of old systems, and archaic beliefs to be turned inside out. It is that strength that is fueling feminism, equality, more compassion for all humans, rights for animals, ethical and sustainable living and lifestyle choices, and practices like meditation and herbal medicine to become mainstream.

**Grab onto that passion of yours, be it:**

- rescuing animals
- fighting for no kill shelters
- feeding and helping the homeless
- jailing men who abuse women and children
- stopping human trafficking
- environmental pollution
- saving the rainforests
- sustainable living practices
- helping 3rd world countries
- promoting fair healthcare
- opening a yoga or meditation studio
- teaching holistic and natural health

- learning and teaching others how to make natural medicine instead of relying on potentially harmful pharmaceutical products and pills.
- providing loving, safe child or pet daycare centers for working mothers
- placing a warm meal in front of a homeless veteran
- showing a struggling child how to read a story or solve a math problem
- visiting the local shelter to play with the animals waiting for a loving home
- marching for the rights of others to vote, work, worship, exist in peace and safety
- use your business savvy to structure fairness in business practices
- use your legal training to bring justice
- use your medical training to overthrow greed and return to healing
- use your political influence to rid our society of power hungry individuals and industries
- etc, etc, etc.

Whatever your passion is, it will be your piece of the puzzle to help bring corrective balance to the world.

This is no time to be quiet and shy or lack confidence. Now more than ever we need to use all of the knowledge and tools available to us to step out of our old roles and into our true Divine Feminine potential. Each of us, like cells in the human body, carry a special piece of the energy that makes up the greater whole. The outside world can affect us, and we can affect it. Put your time and efforts into promoting what you love.

There is nothing that can't be fixed, changed or saved when we have the powers from within and divine assistance to guide us. However you reach the heavens and they reach back to you, through prayer, meditation, journeying, dreams or intuition, makes no differences, it is all the same, use everything you have to reach your full potential as a Divine Feminine.

One of my favorite old Chinese proverbs is "There are many paths to the top of the mountain, but when you get there the view is always the same". Meaning there is no one "right" way for everyone to accomplish the same outcome.

There are many ways to accomplish the same end. So be sure to cheer your sisters on in their work, even if it looks different than yours. Divine Feminine Energy is about tolerance, love and acceptance of those who are different than you are. A good heart is a good heart, don't judge. They will have influence and reach people you can't.

Do not doubt yourself or your ability to contribute to the betterment of the world. We are creative beings and we were each born with gifts. What is your gift to earth?

As women establish themselves as local and global leaders, this positive Divine Feminine Energy will be able to quickly spread to women and men of all races and nationalities. The result will see the planet adopting a new reality and entering the new era of the embracing, inclusive, nurturing heart of humanity.

Find your passion, your contribution and reason for being on earth at this time and begin contributing to the betterment of the world, your community and churches. The Divine Feminine will bring corrective balance into the world because when we see pain, suffering and injustice we will do something about it.

*"We need more effort to promote basic human values, human compassion, human affection. And in that respect, females have more sensitivity for others pain and suffering" Dalai Lama*

# CONCLUSION

*"If you don't know history, then you don't know anything. You are a leaf that doesn't know it is part of a tree." Michael Crichton*

I hope you have found something in this book which has touched your heart and resonated with your soul to remind you of your divinity and help you overcome self-doubt and bring hope and joy into your life. There is no reason to have fear or self doubt when you know who you are; which is a divine feminine being, a decedent of ancient divine mothers and grandmothers, and a unique being unlike any other with your own unique purpose.

Remember and honor the legacy of your ancient Divine Feminine ancestors. A woman with this knowledge can confidently change herself and the world. When you know and understand your past, you feel more rooted and connected to something bigger. A woman armed with love and ancestral wisdom is an unstoppable force. No one exists alone, no one lives alone. We are all who we are because others were who they were.

Bring back the wisdom that women carried. Break free from the old stories and the lies we have been told that we are not enough in so many ways.

Even though some of us have supportive friends and family members, our inner experience is that we're alone in our restlessness and our full flourishing is a personal journey we have to tackle by ourselves. Many of us have spent decades struggling in isolation, trying to break free from old patterns and beliefs ingrained in us since childhood. You need to find groups, organizations and women's circles of like-minded women for support, friendship and education.

As Divine Feminine we have to take responsibility for our actions, decisions, how we allow people to treat us, our health, happiness, freedom, power and well-being. We either take control of our lives or allow others to continue to control us.

Regardless of your circumstances or situation you can acknowledge your Divinity, develop your Divine Feminine Energy and skills, improve or change your life and prepare yourself to begin to contribute your unique part in improving and healing yourself and the world around you.

Right now Divine Feminine Energy is returning to our society where greater equality between men and women is being established. At this moment, we have more female leaders than we ever have in the history of our planet. And not only this, but both men and women are beginning to lead with compassion and heart-felt thinking.

The last few generations of women were so busy trying to prove they can do anything a man can do and they are losing their uniqueness and femininity. Many have become angry and impatient for change and feel they need to be loud and aggressive to be heard. Women are equal to men but different, to our advantage. As Divine Feminine were created to do everything a man can't do.

We are being asked to work with loving and gentle Divine Feminine Energy in order to build a society where peace, harmony, and compassion are upheld. We are ready to stand beside the Divine Masculine so that we may work together in unity and balance.

Divine Feminine Energy is not to oppose the masculine energy but will attempt to bring it into balance with humane behavior and reverence for all humans, nature and the earth. It will be an uphill battle and the masculine will not change or relinquish their control easily, but it is slowly happening as the Divine Feminine overcome their self doubt and rise above the thousands of years of being held back and told they are not enough.

When you tap into your Divine Feminine Energy, you will awaken to new possibilities and birth a greater level of creativity in your life. By channeling your Inner Goddess, your relationships will become more loving and nurturing. You will experience a deeper sense of personal freedom and self-love. In no uncertain terms, you will have a spiritual awakening and a surge of self-confidence.

My only intent for writing this book is to pass on knowledge to help you remember your Divinity, your specialness, your femaleness, and your self-worth, so that you may over come self-doubt and never feel less than anyone else or feel you have to take a back seat to anyone, ever again.

To be continued in Volume II, *Awakening Your Inner Goddess*.....

# RESOURCES & REFERENCES

**Ancient Ancestral Foods and Celebrations:**
GatherVictoria.com

**Energy Medicine:**
Energy Medicine, Donna Eden
Vibrational Medicine, Richard Gerber
The Emotion Code, Bradley Nelson

**Fiction for Fun:**
The Mists of Avalon, Marion Zimmer Bradley
The Celestine Prophecy, James Redfield
Gaia Codex, Sarah Drew

**Labyrinths:**
My Exploration of Labyrinths, Alex B. Champion
LabyrinthLocator.com (worldwide locator)

**Medicine Wheels:**
The Medicine Wheel: Path of the Heart, Donata Ahern

**Meditation:**
Walking Meditation, Nguyen Anh-Huong & Thich Nhat Hanh
Becoming Supernatural, Dr. Joe Dispensa

**Nature:**
Forest Bathing, Dr. Qng
OneWillowApothecaries.com, Asia Suler

**Pendulums:**
Pendulum Magic for Beginners, Richard Webster
The Book of Pendulum Healing, Joun Rose Staffen
The Beginners Guide to Pendulum Dowsing, Brenda Hunt

**Religion:**
10 Lies the Church Tells Women, J. Lee Grady

**Science:**
The Biology of Belief, Bruce Lipton
Human by Design, Gregg Braden

**Shamanism:**
Change Your Story, Change Your Life: Using Shamanic and
Jungian Tools to Achieve Personal Transformation, Carl Greer
Awaking to the Spirit World, Sandra Ingerman
Shamanic Journeying, Sandra Ingerman
Shaman, Healer, Sage, Albert Villodo
TheFourWindsSociety.com, Albert Villodo

**Wellness**
Grow a New Body, Albert Villodo
Ancient Secret of The Fountain of Youth, Peter Kelder

**Women's Prehistory:**
When God Was a Woman, Merlin Stone
When Drummers Were Women, Layne Redmond
Invisible Women of Prehistory, Judy Foster
The Great Cosmic Mother, Monica Sjoo & Barbara Mor
The Living Goddess, Morija Gymbustas
A Woman in the Shaman's Body, Barbara Tedlock, PhD

# ABOUT THE AUTHOR

Marilyn Pabon is a dedicated researcher in all areas of natural health and wellness and ancient ancestral wisdom. She is passionate about supporting women in ways that will be the most relevant and useful for them in today's world.

She has worked for both medical and natural health practitioners, has had her own practice as a Holistic Nutrition Consultant, Energy Worker and Detoxification Facilitator. She has taught medical doctors how to integrate natural modalities into their practices and writes for newspapers and magazines.

Her mission now is to help women harness divine health, their own creative power, self esteem and personal potential so they may become the Divine Feminine they are meant to be. For this goal she has written a series of four books and created online courses to help her divine feminine sisters find their Inner Goddesses and live to their full potential.

For more information about Marilyn Pabon and her work, visit www.marilynpabon.com

# SHARE THE DREAM

*Divine Feminine Handbook* I, II, III, and IV are more than a set of books.

It is a lifestyle and movement in which modern women can live to their greatest and truest versions of themselves. It's a dedication to empower women to break free from the shackles of outdated and limiting beliefs. It is a call to awaken the Divine Feminine Energy in us all. It is a remembrance of our divine ancient foremothers who once were revered as creators of life, healers, spiritual guides, shamans and leaders.

Please share these books if you too have a dream of helping your divine sisters learn of their sacred heritage and cultivate their inner goddesses, so they too can live empowered fulfilling lives.

One of the simplest ways you can do that is by leaving a review online. Write down your thoughts about the book on your favorite book selling or review sites so that other Divine Feminine women can be inspired to know more.

You can also share your ideas on your social media page. Make sure to include the official hashtag: #divinefemininehandbook.

From my heart to yours,
Marilyn Pabon

Printed in the United States
by Baker & Taylor Publisher Services